Coloring Book of Vintage Caricatures and Characters

Publisher's Note

Mix-BooksOnline.com

Manufactured in the United States.

Table of Contents

Introduction

In 1941, Mitchell Smith's classic guide to creating caricatures and cartoons was published. Smith's aim was to produce a concise treatise on the art of caricaturing and he included many caricatures of famous men of the day. We've taken those plates, plus others that illustrate such things as Expressions or Action and cleaned them up by eliminating stray marks and other errors so that you can color them and make them your own.

Not all the original plates were suitable for coloring so we've added some vintage advertising images to make 47 pages of illustrations in all. Each of these illustrated pages has a blank back side so you can cut them out and not be concerned about bleed-through.
Smith's book, The Art of Caricaturing, and the vintage ad illustrations are all in the public domain.

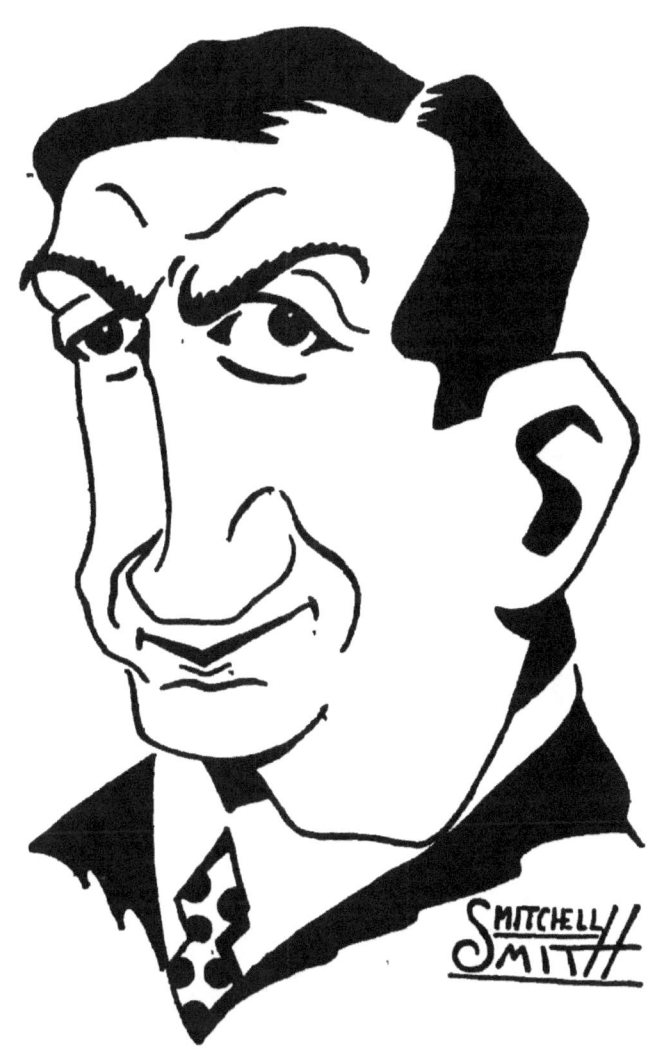

NICOLA

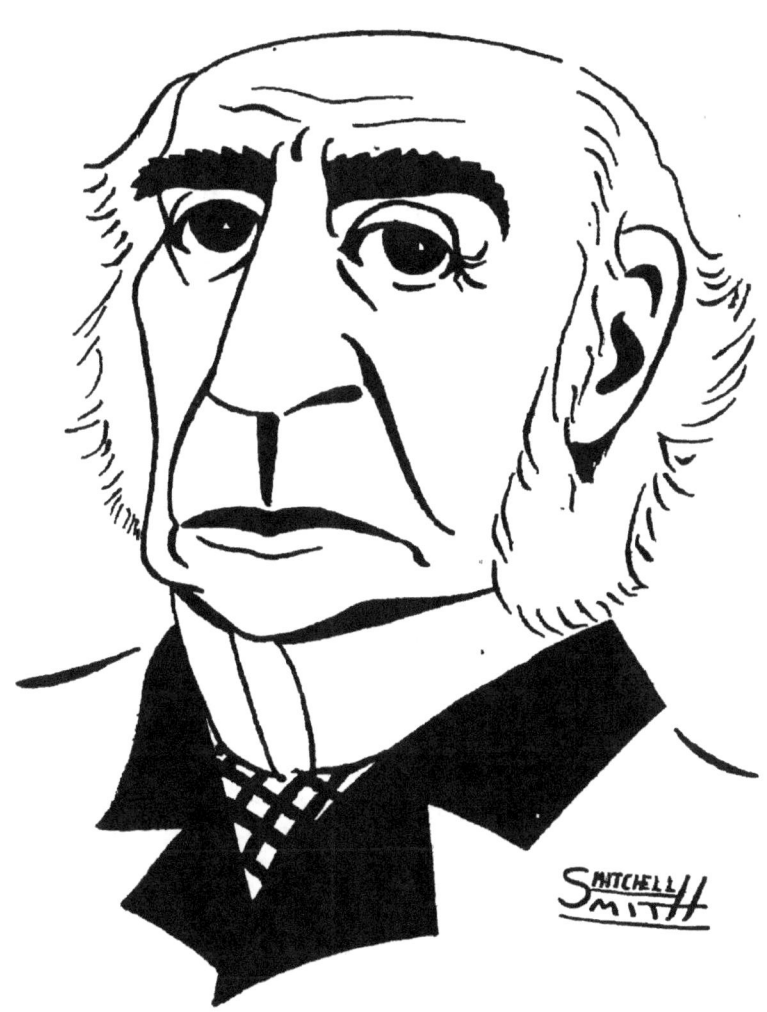

GLADSTONE

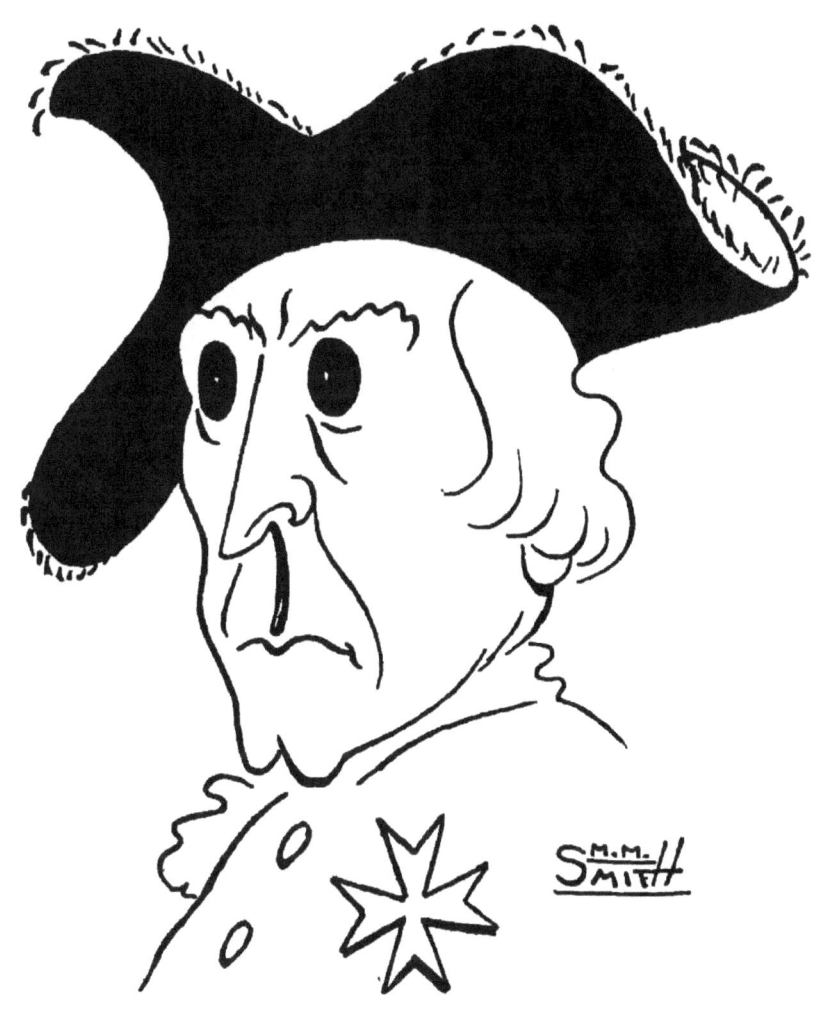

FREDERICK THE GREAT

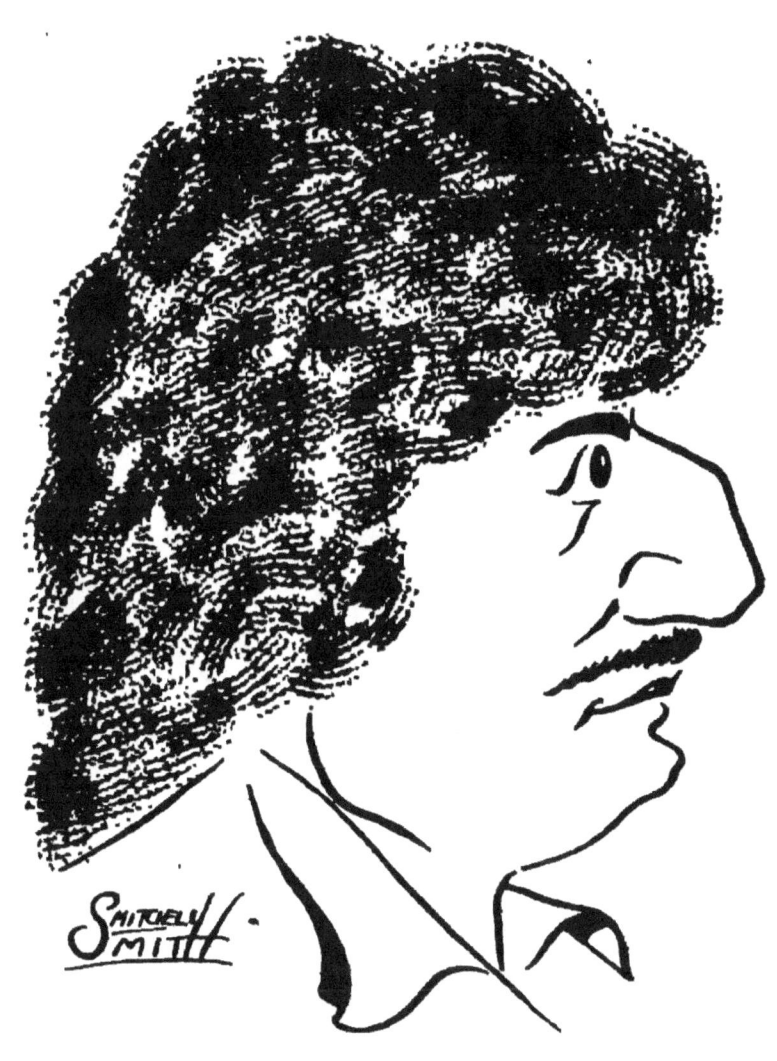

HERRICK

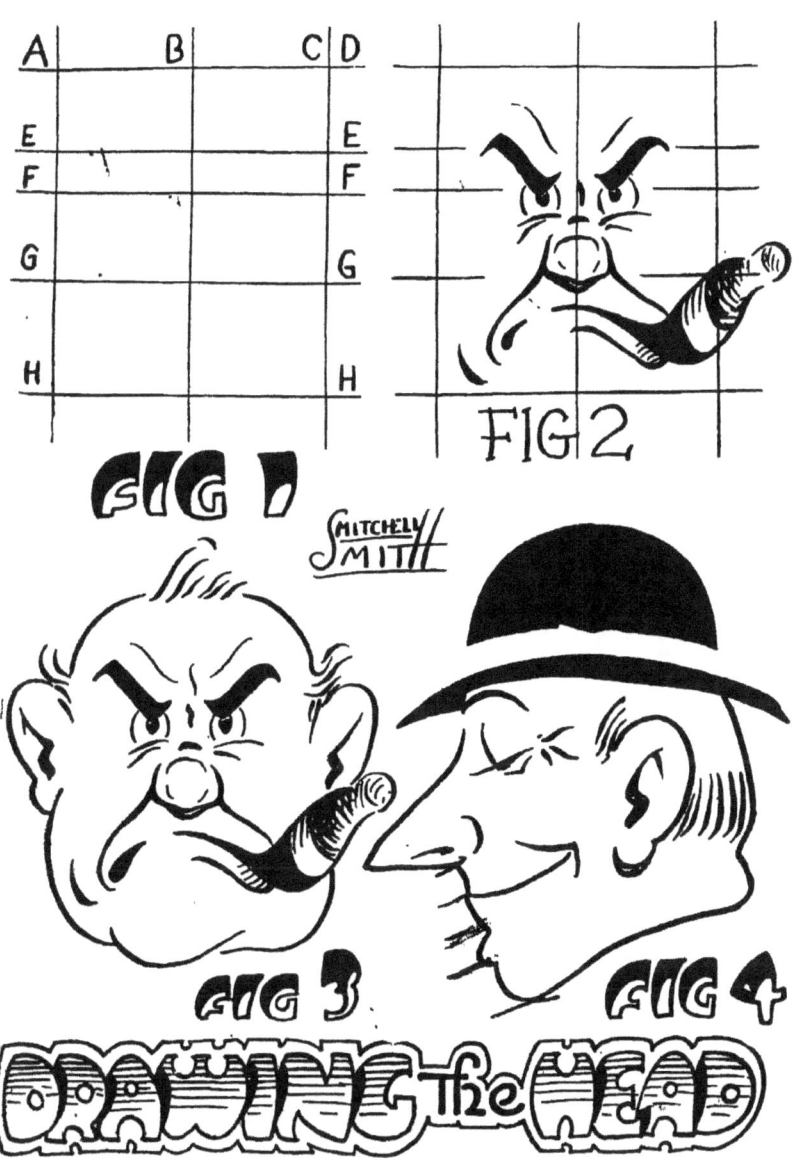

PLATE 2

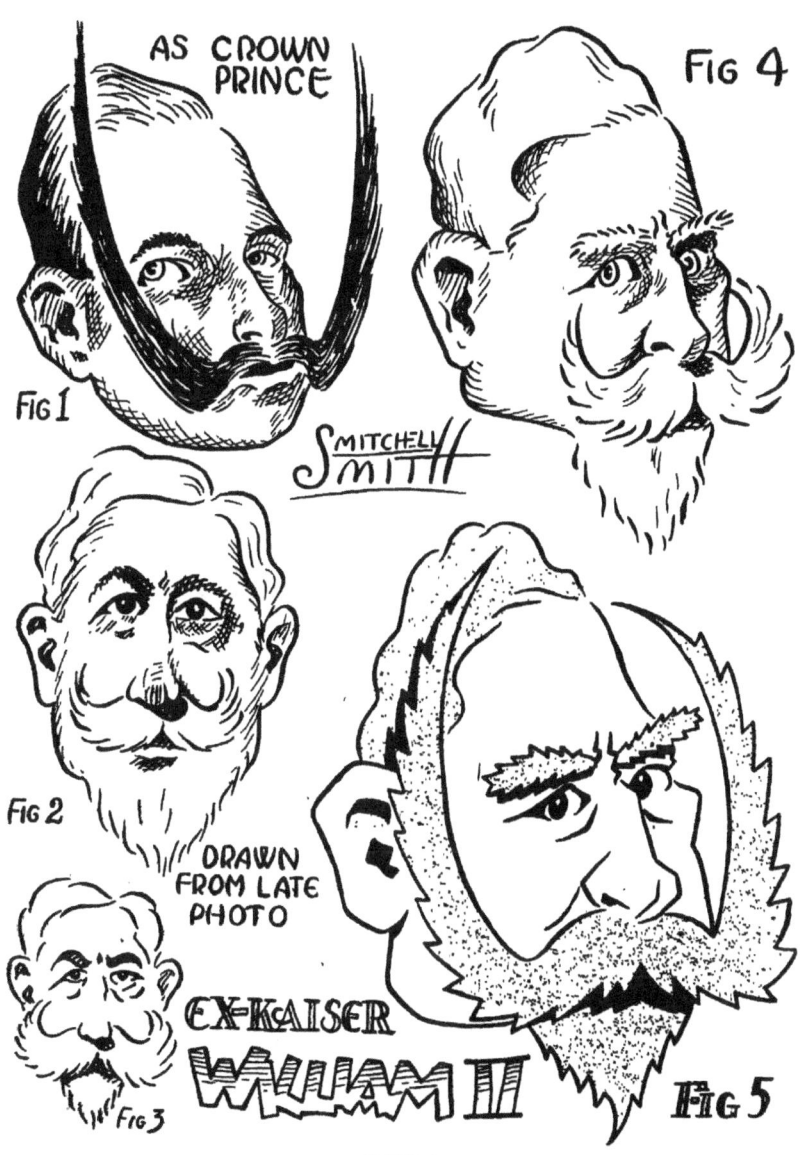

AS CROWN PRINCE

FIG 4

FIG 1

MITCHELL SMITH

FIG 2

DRAWN FROM LATE PHOTO

FIG 3

EX-KAISER WILLIAM II

FIG 5

PLATE 3

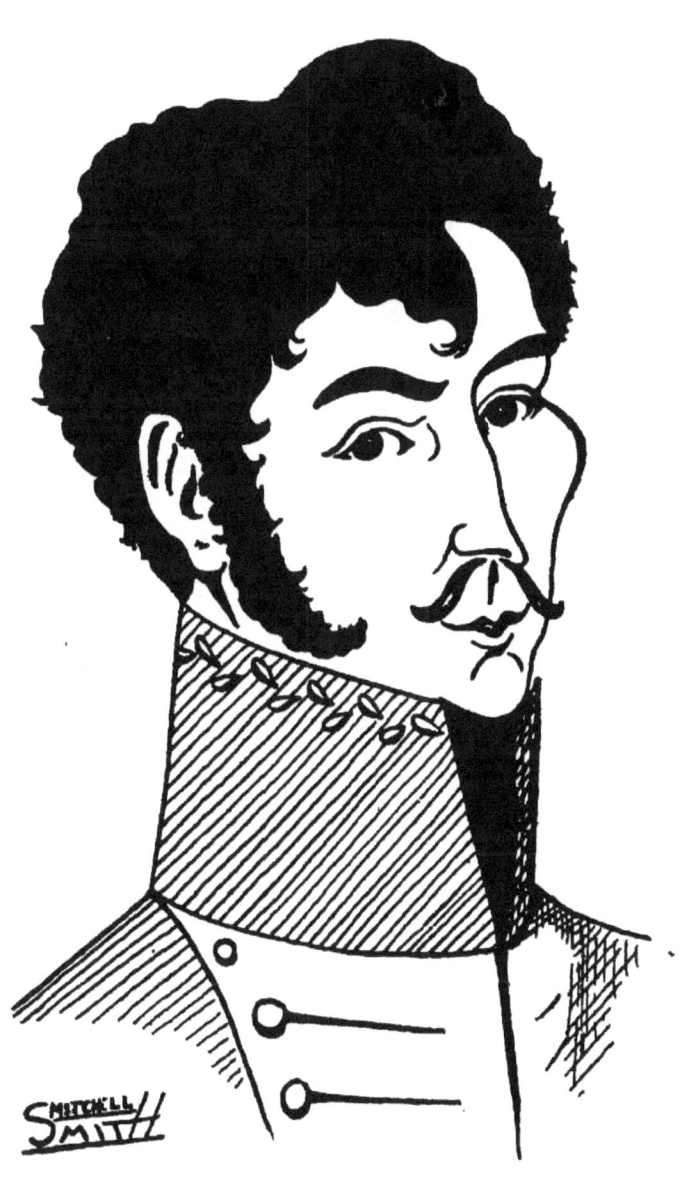

BOLIVAR

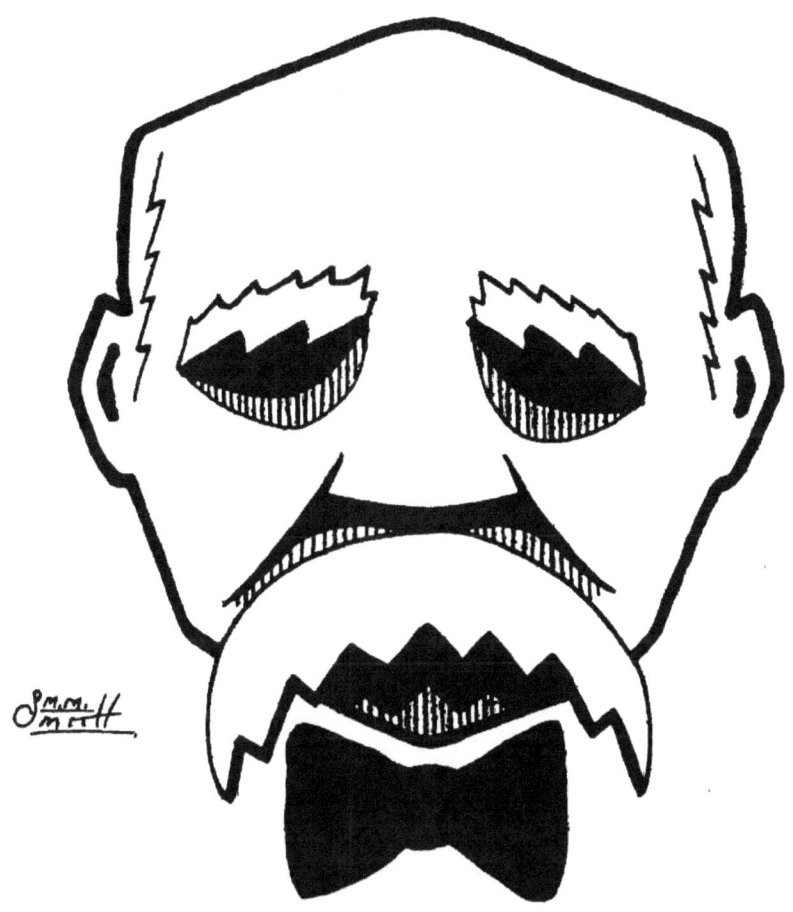

CLEMENCEAU

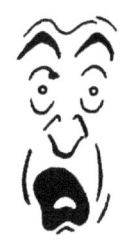
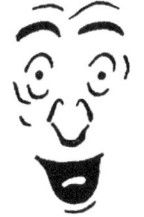
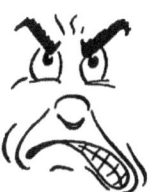
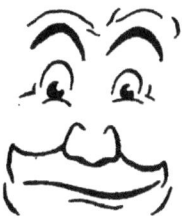

FRIGHT SURPRISE ANGER ATTENTION

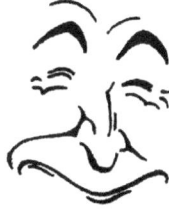
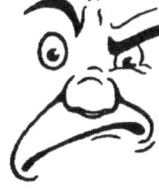
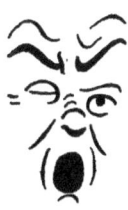
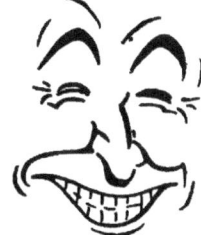

SMILE SNEER PAIN LAUGHTER

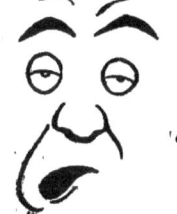
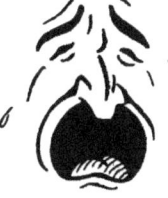
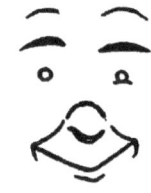
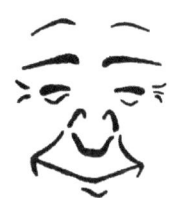

STUPIDITY WEEPING ANTICIPATION CONTENTMENT

EXPRESSIONS

PLATE 4

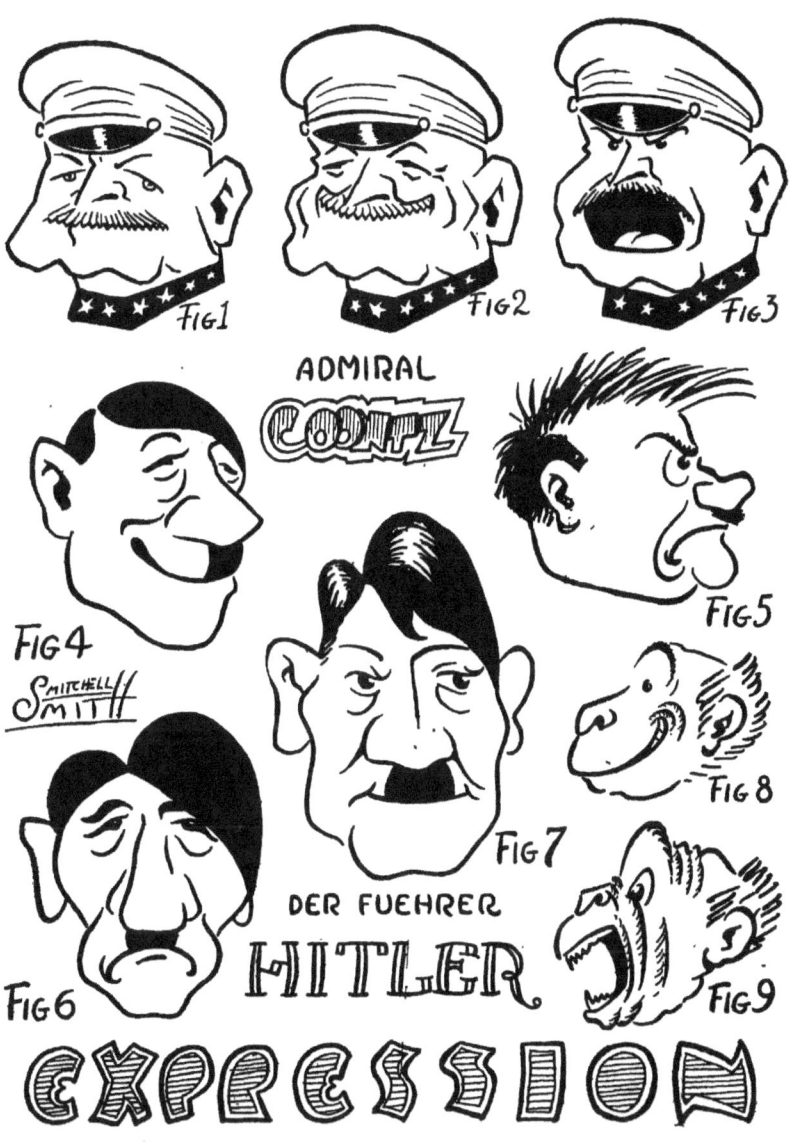

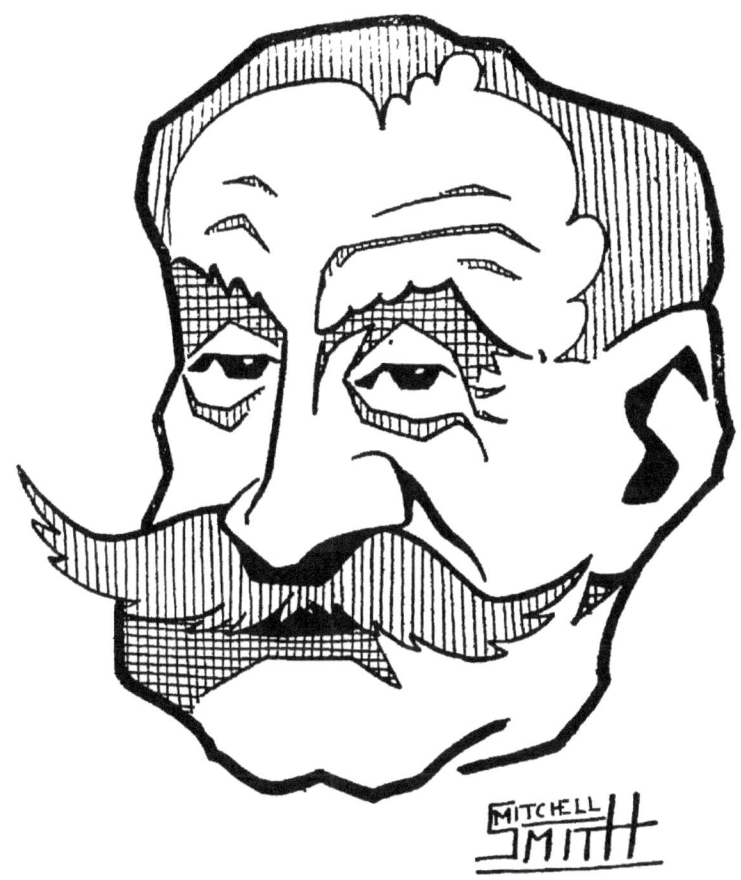

FOCH

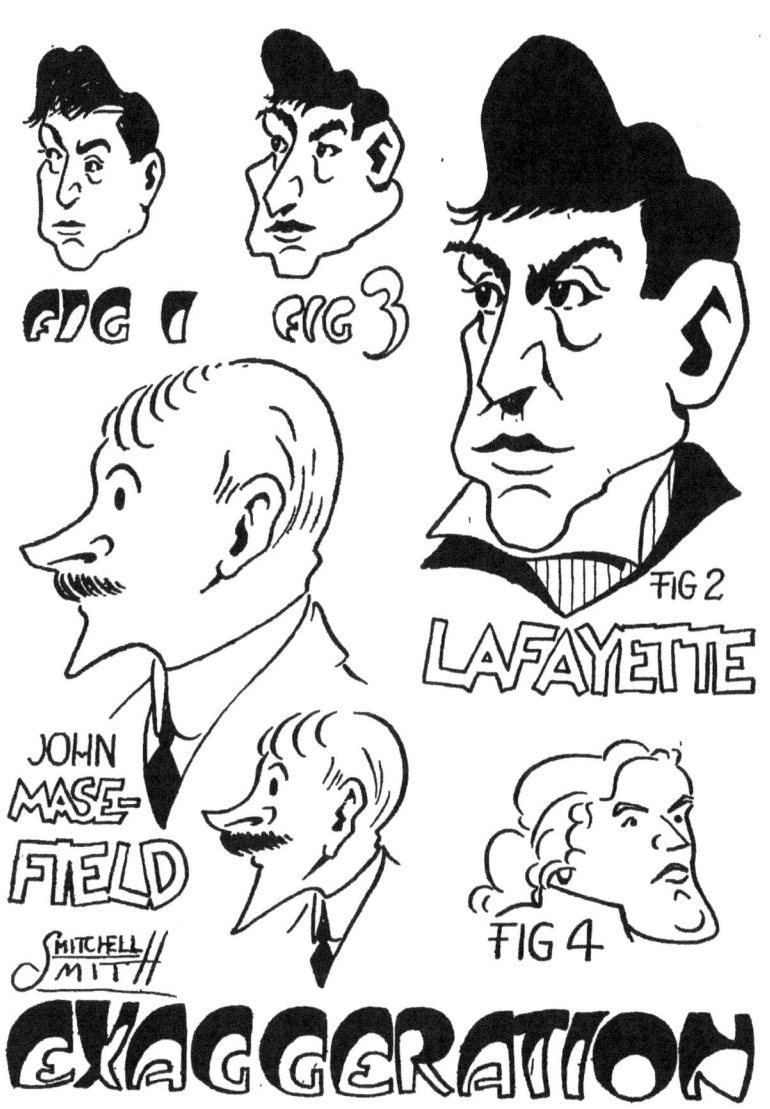

FIG 1

FIG 3

FIG 2

LAFAYETTE

JOHN MASEFIELD

MITCHELL SMITH

FIG 4

EXAGGERATION

PLATE 6

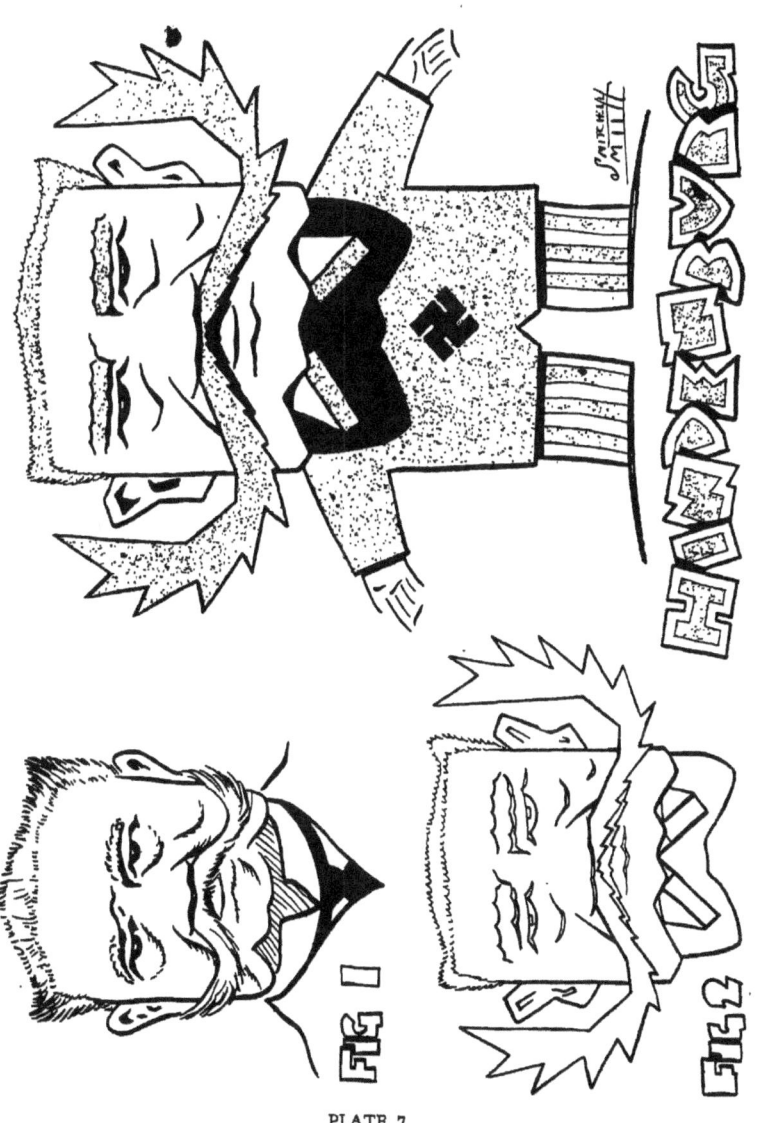

PLATE 7

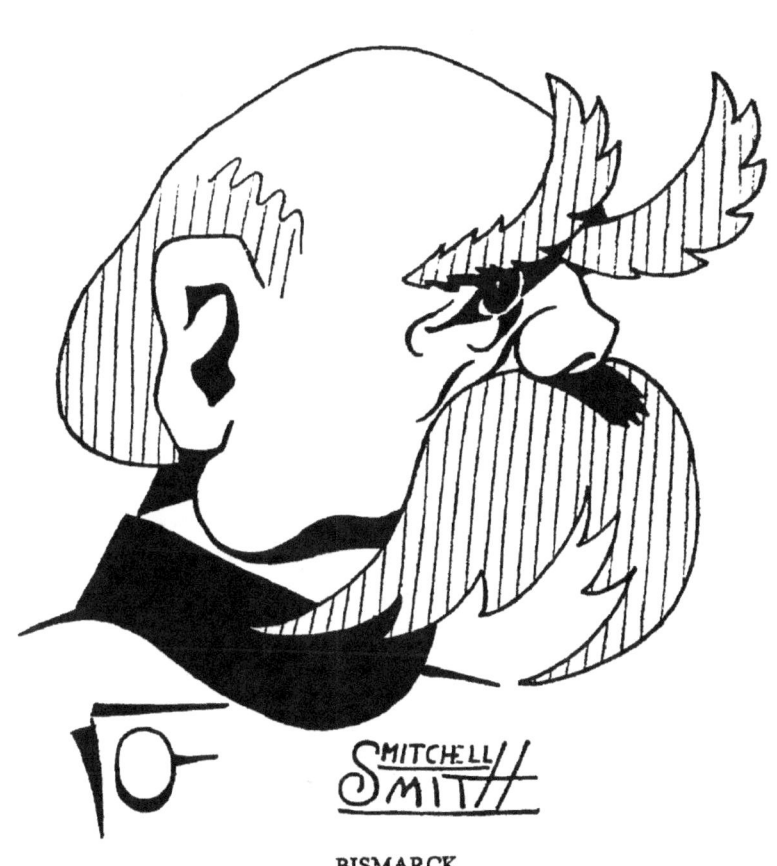

BISMARCK

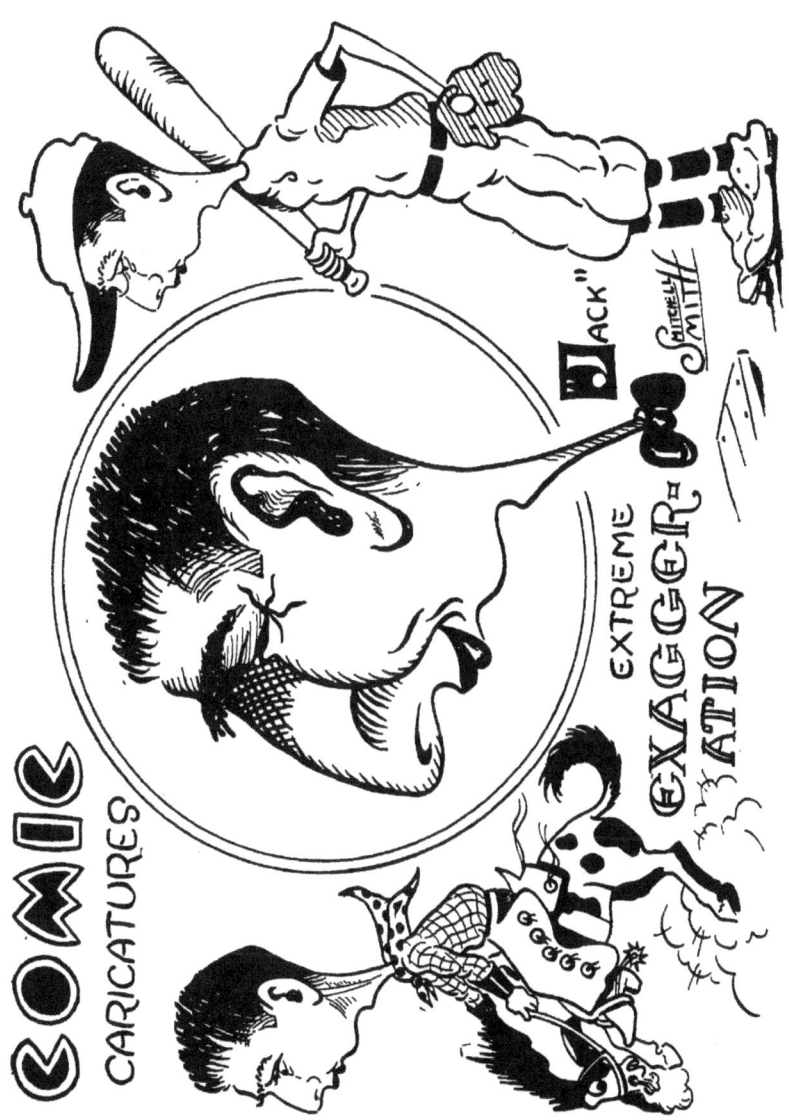

COMIC CARICATURES

"Jack"

MITCHELL SMITH

EXTREME EXAGGERATION

PLATE 8

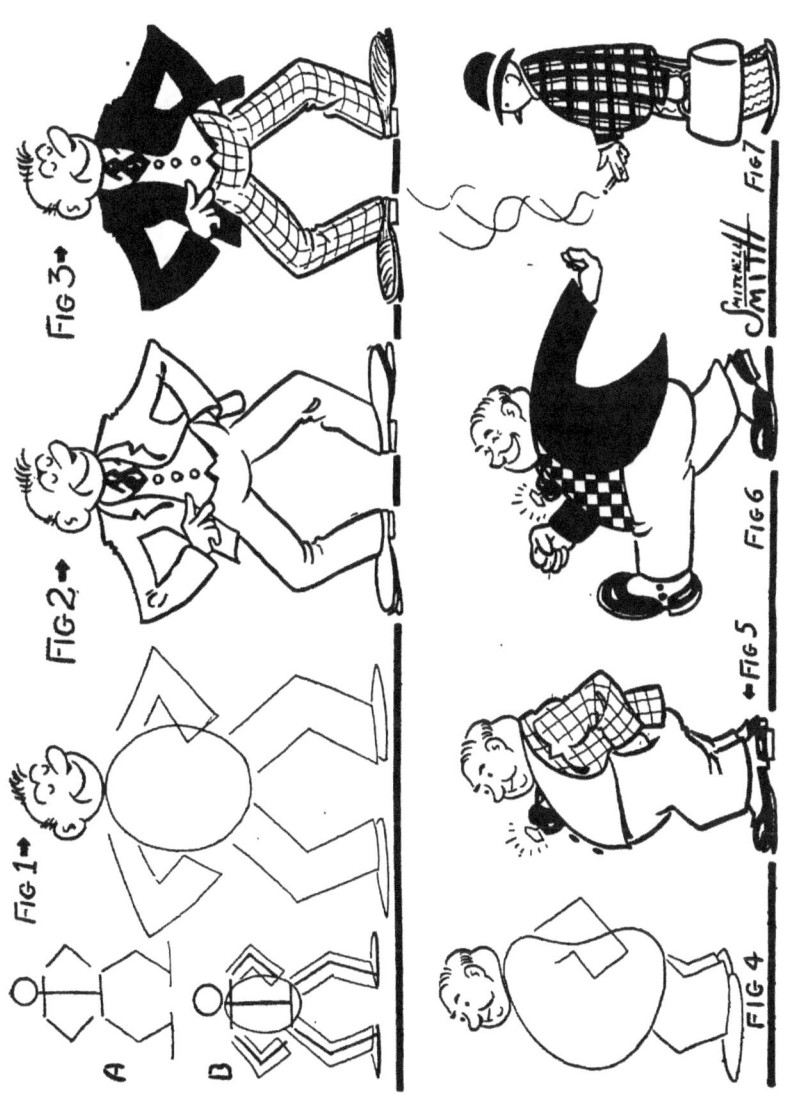

PLATE 9

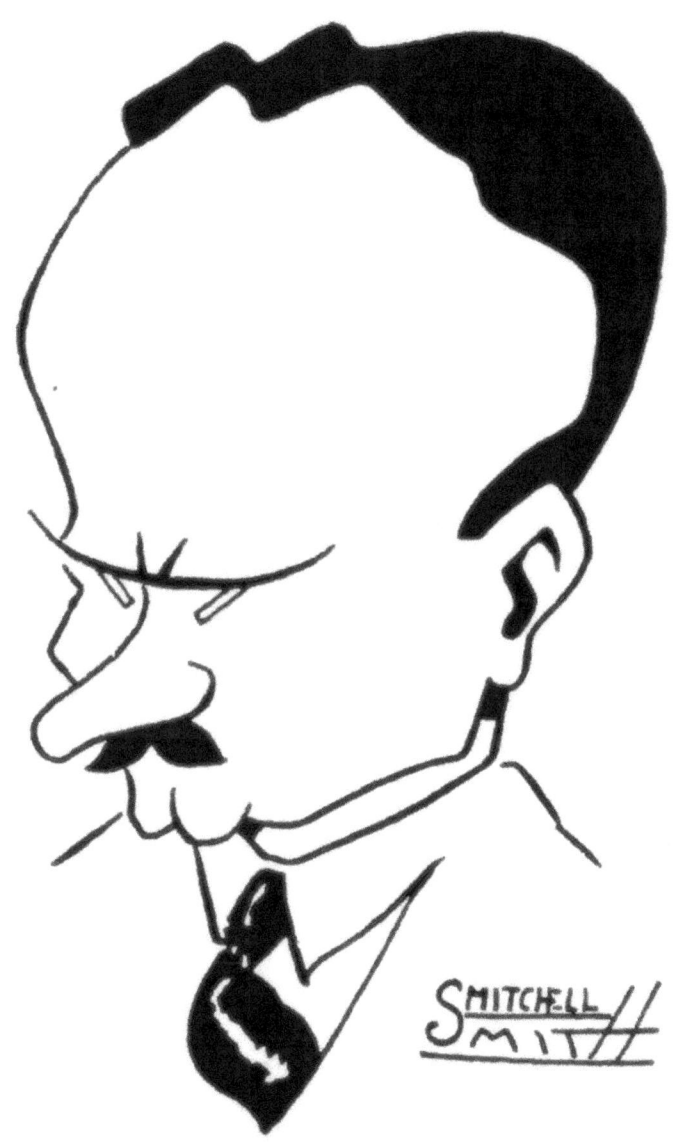

COFFIN

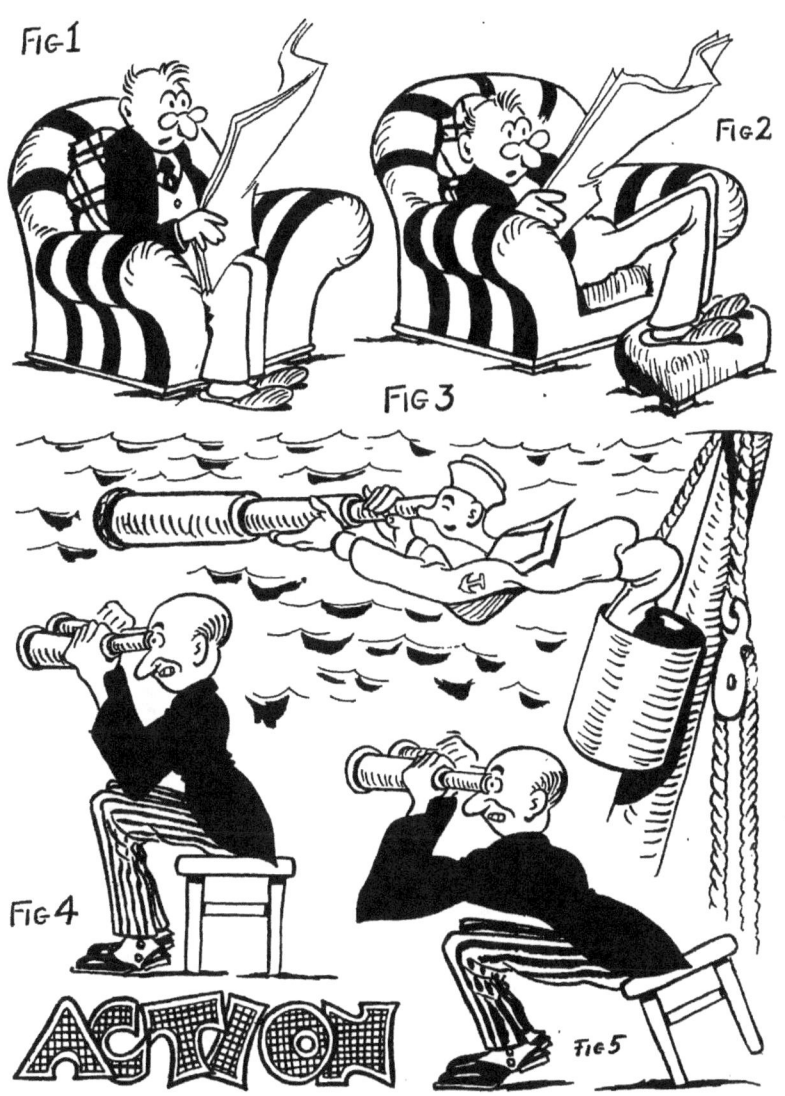

FIG 1

FIG 2

FIG 3

FIG 4

FIG 5

ACTION

PLATE 10

41

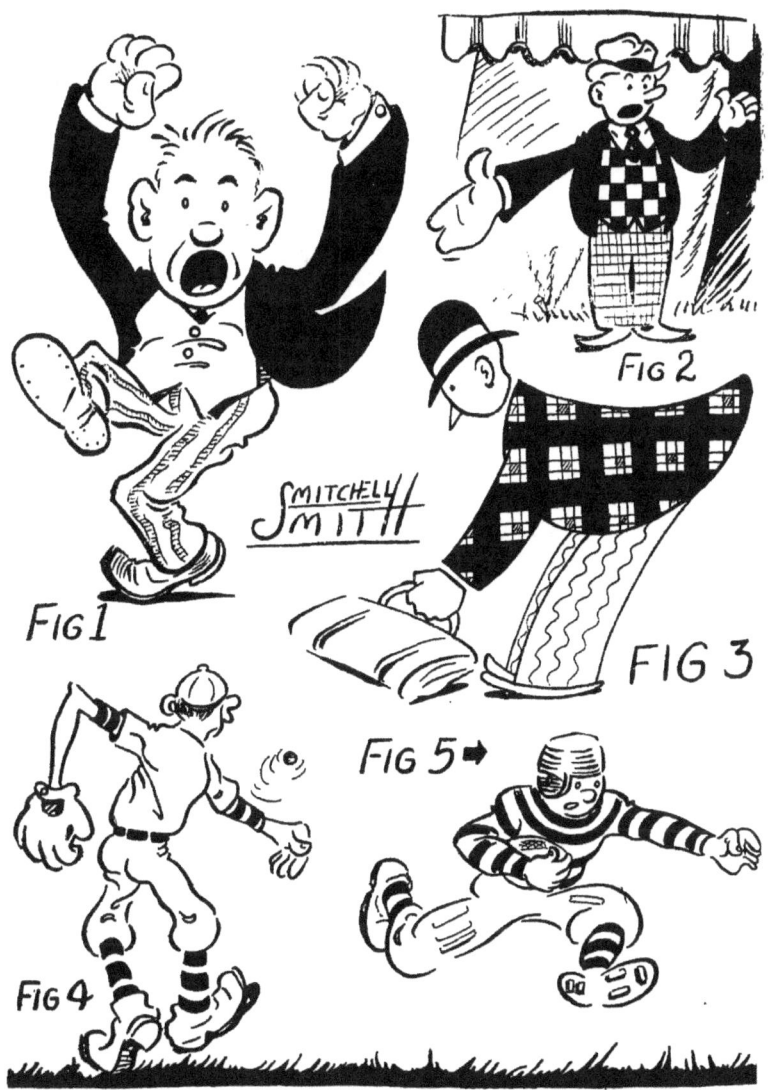

FIG 1

FIG 2

FIG 3

FIG 4

FIG 5 ➡

MITCHELL SMITH

PLATE 11

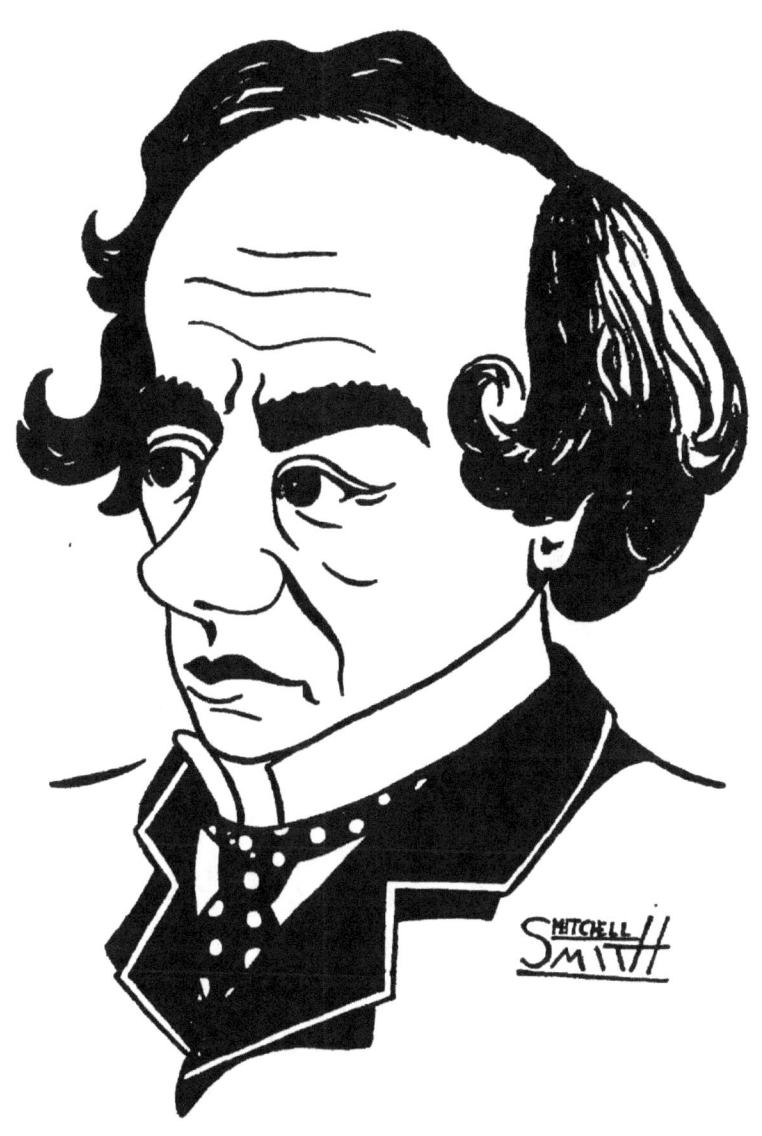

DISRAELI

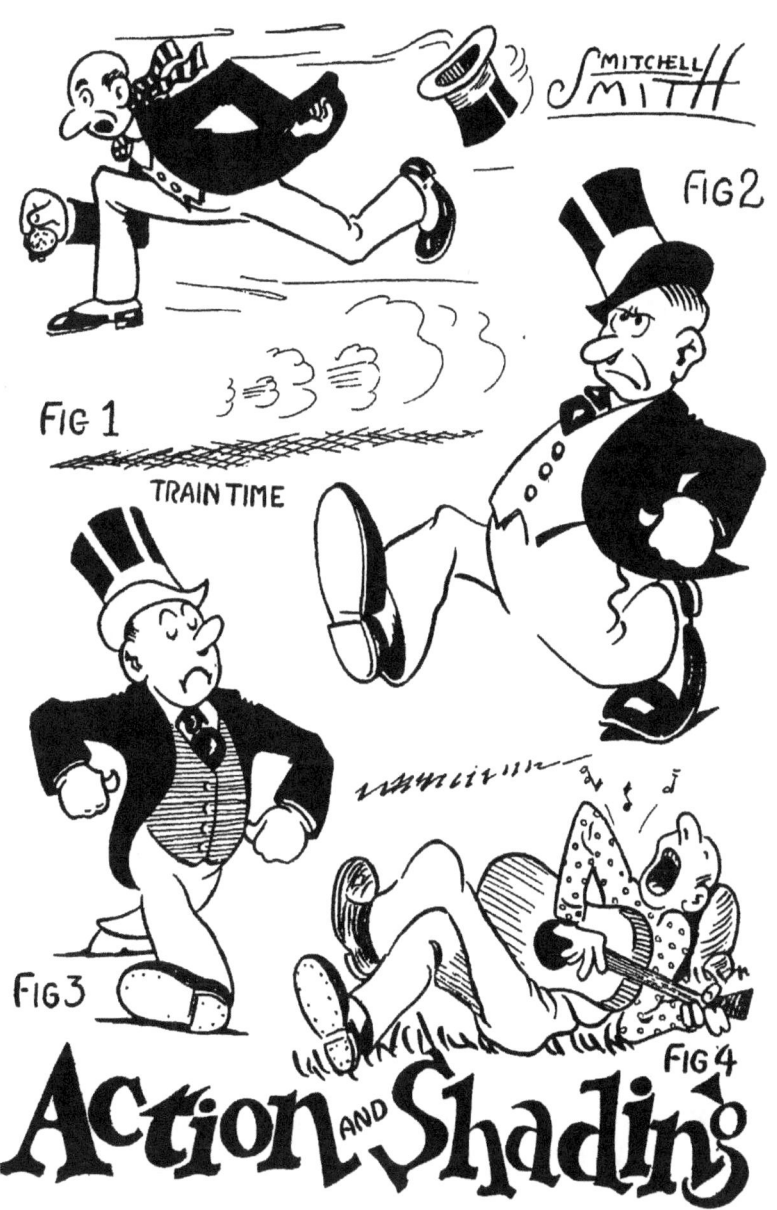

MITCHELL SMITH

FIG 2

FIG 1

TRAIN TIME

FIG 3

FIG 4

Action AND Shading

PLATE 12

47

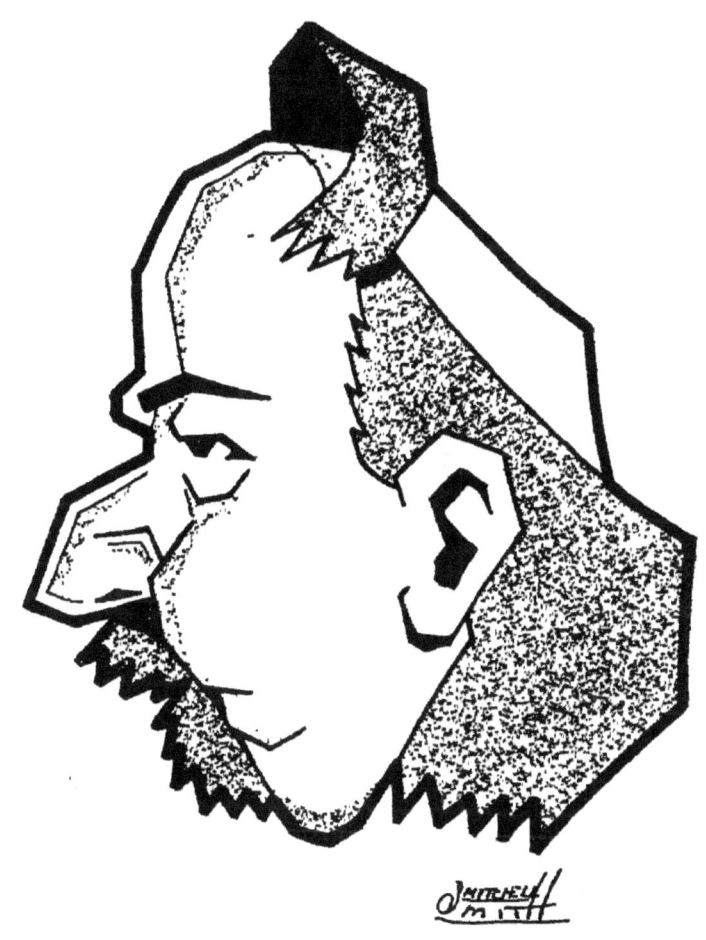

TAFT

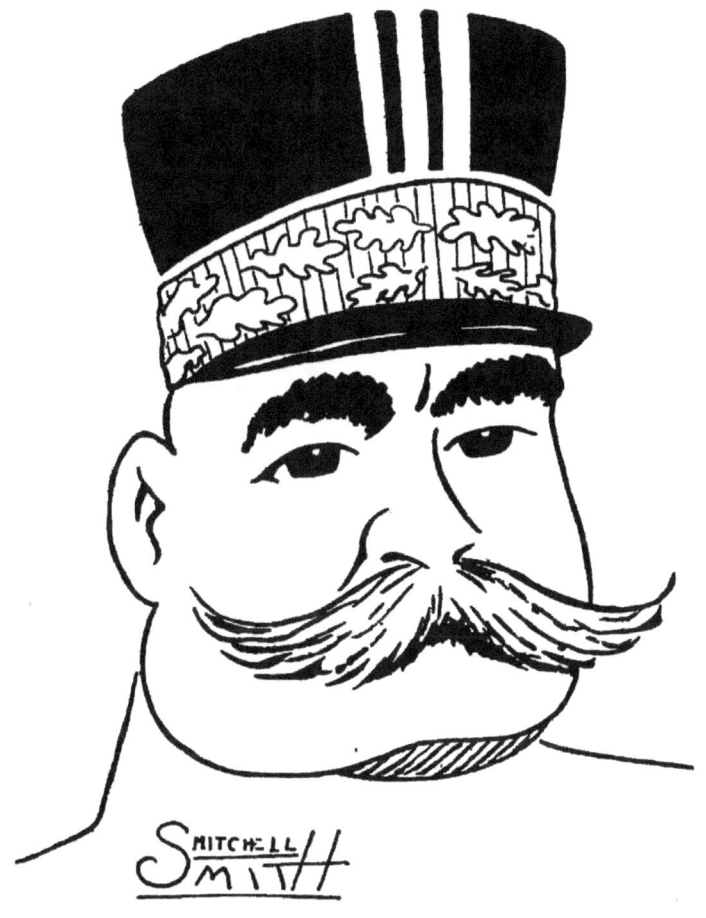

JOFFRE

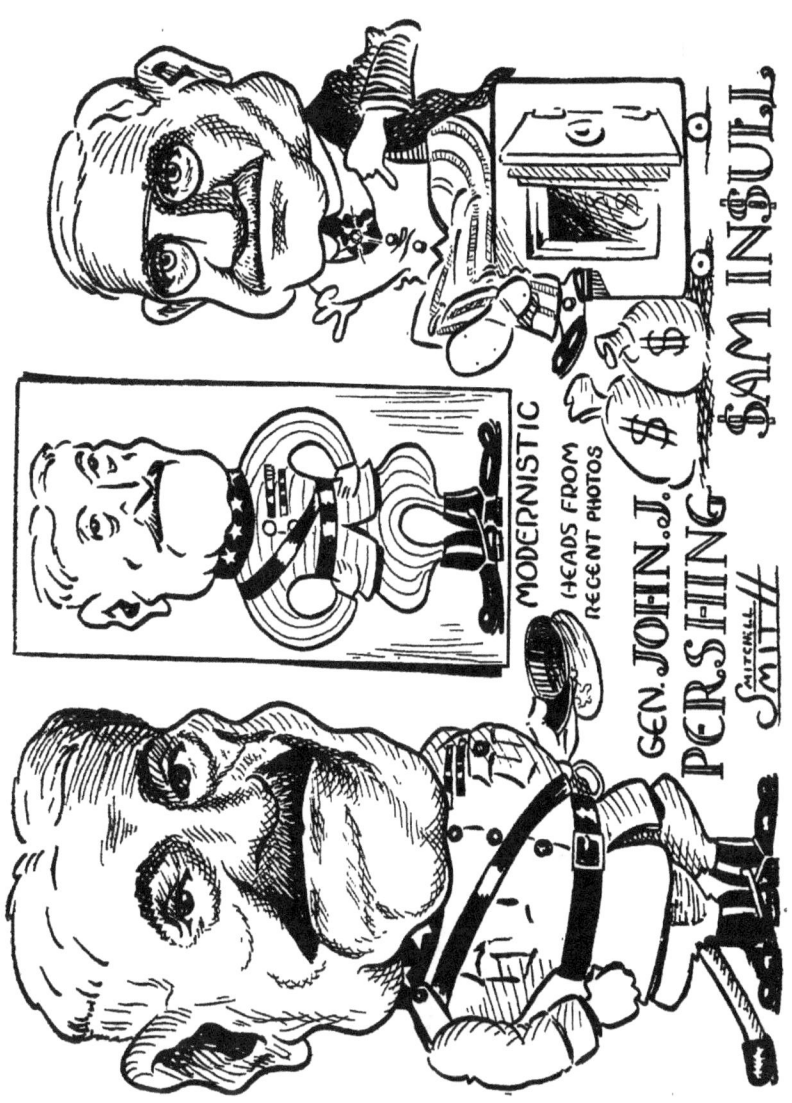

MODERNISTIC
HEADS FROM RECENT PHOTOS

GEN. JOHN J. PERSHING

SAM INSULL $ $ $

MITCHELL SMITH

PLATE 13

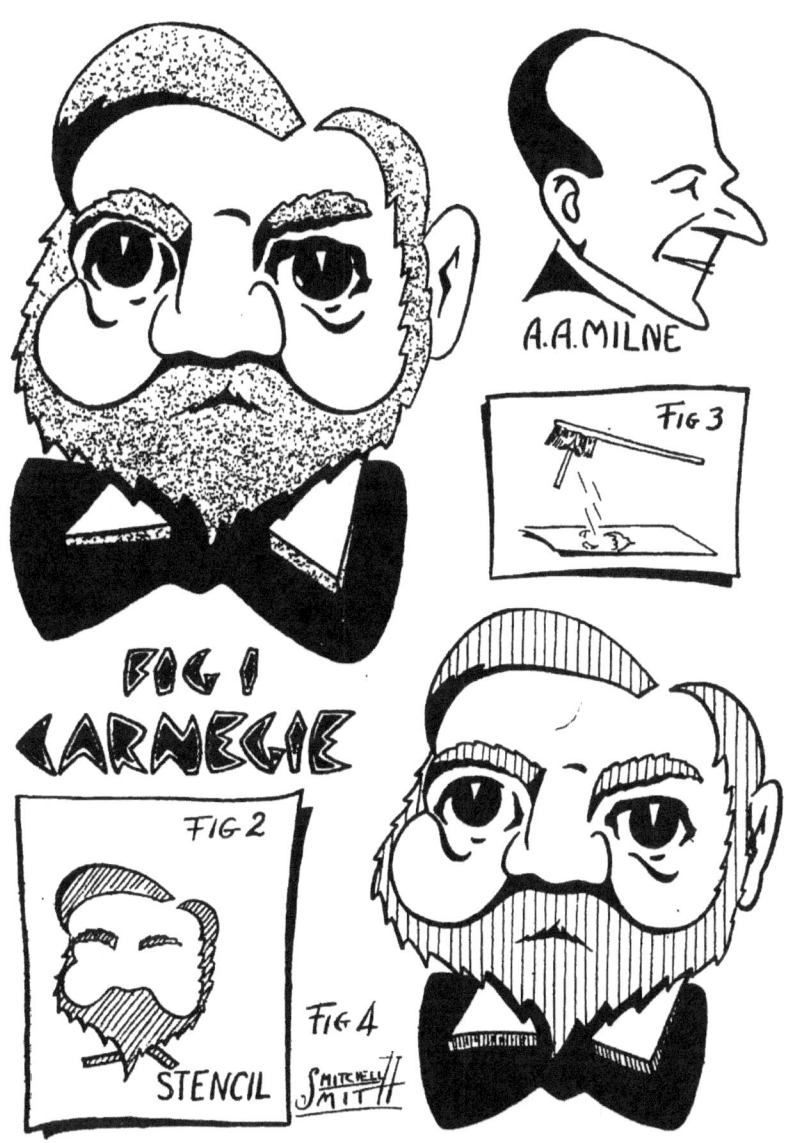

PLATE 14

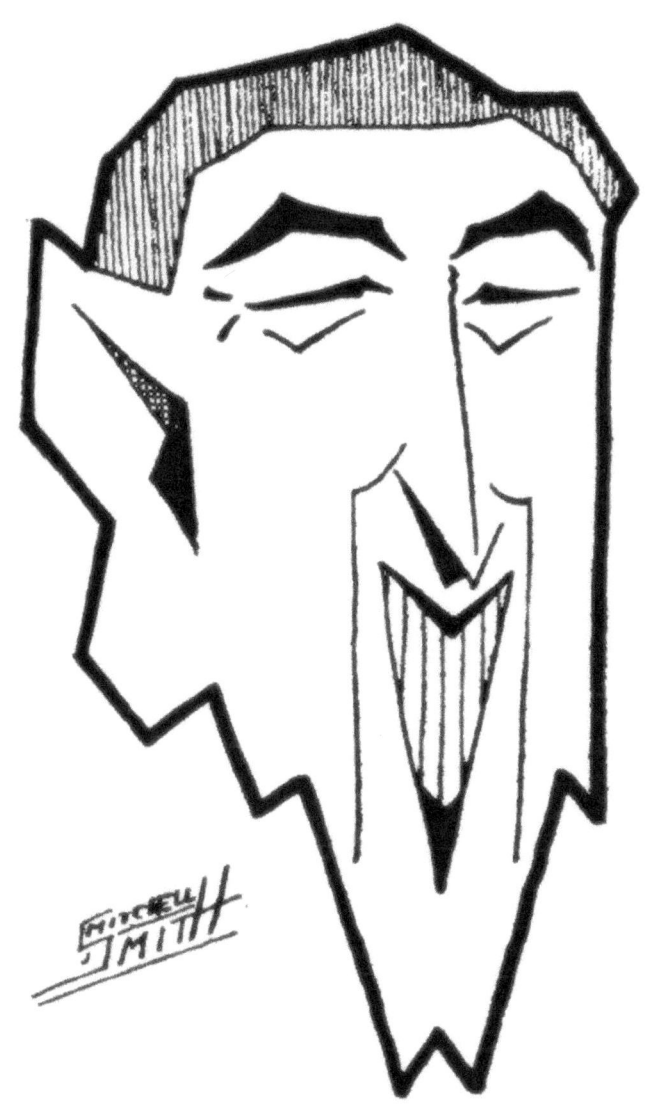

WILSON

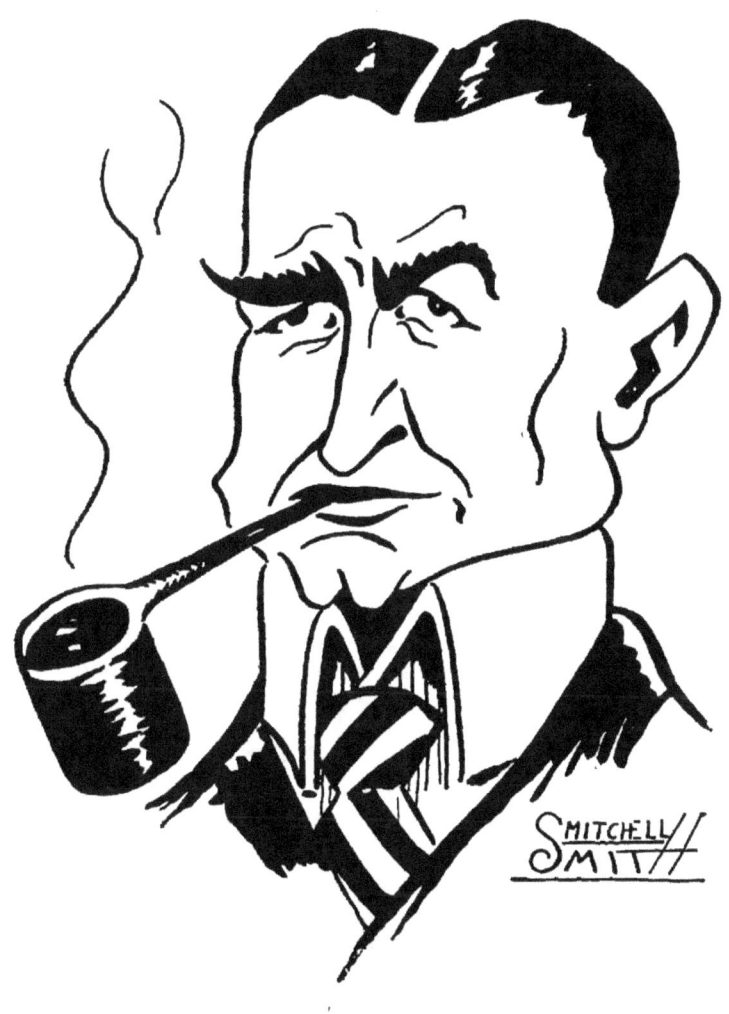

DAWES

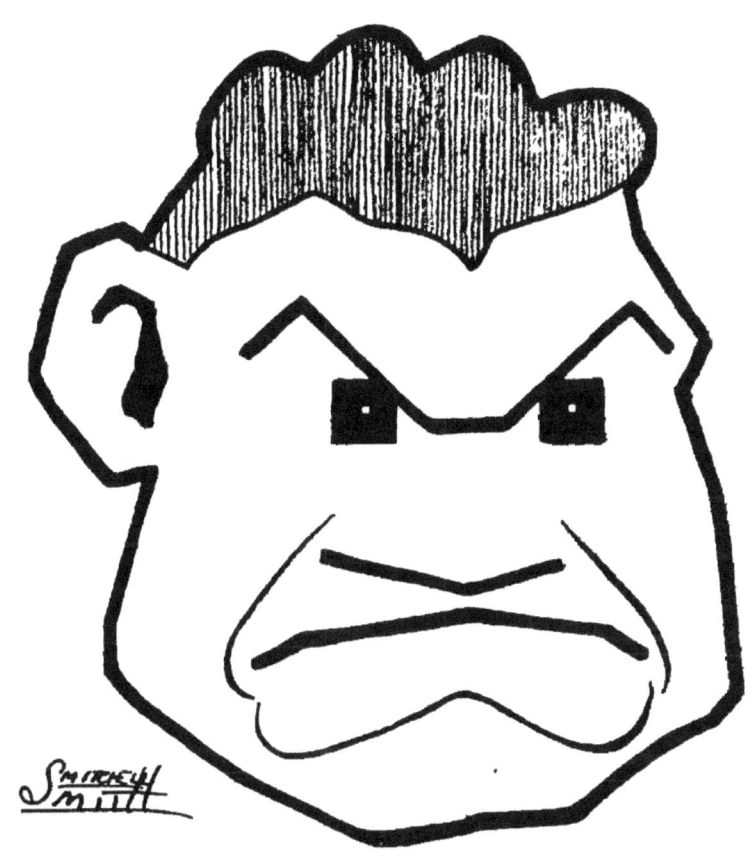

DEMPSEY

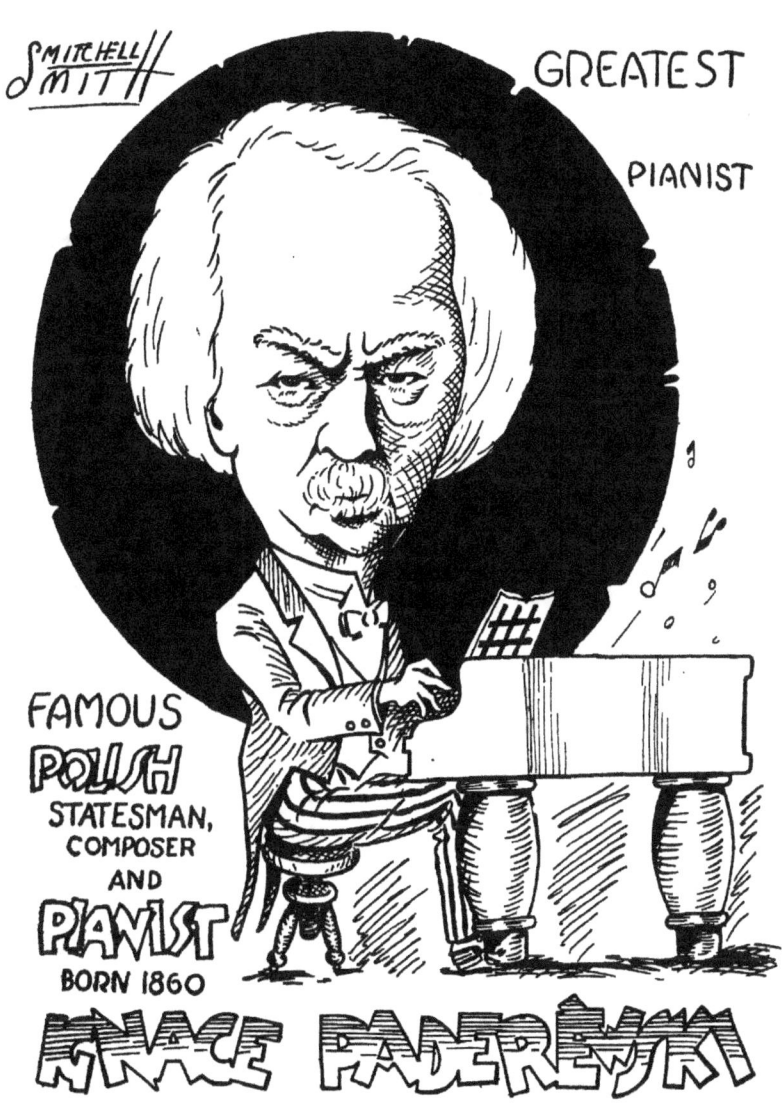

GREATEST

PIANIST

FAMOUS POLISH STATESMAN, COMPOSER AND PIANIST BORN 1860

IGNACE PADEREWSKI

PLATE 16

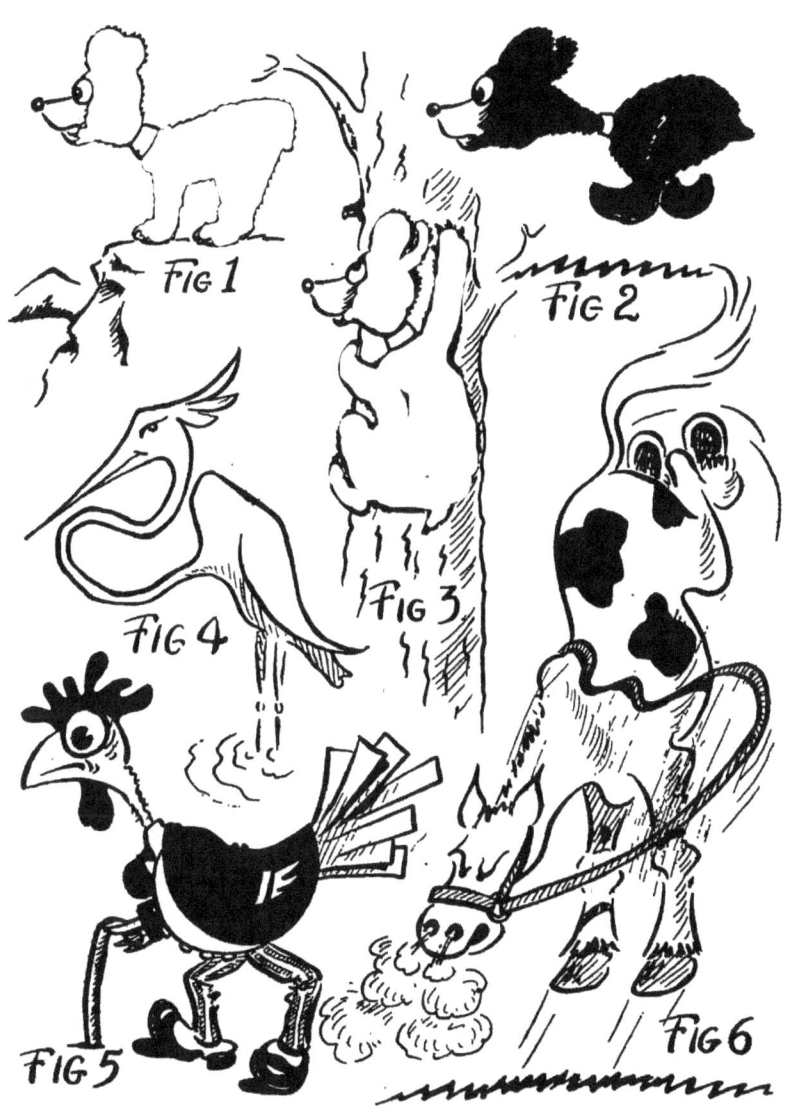

PLATE 17

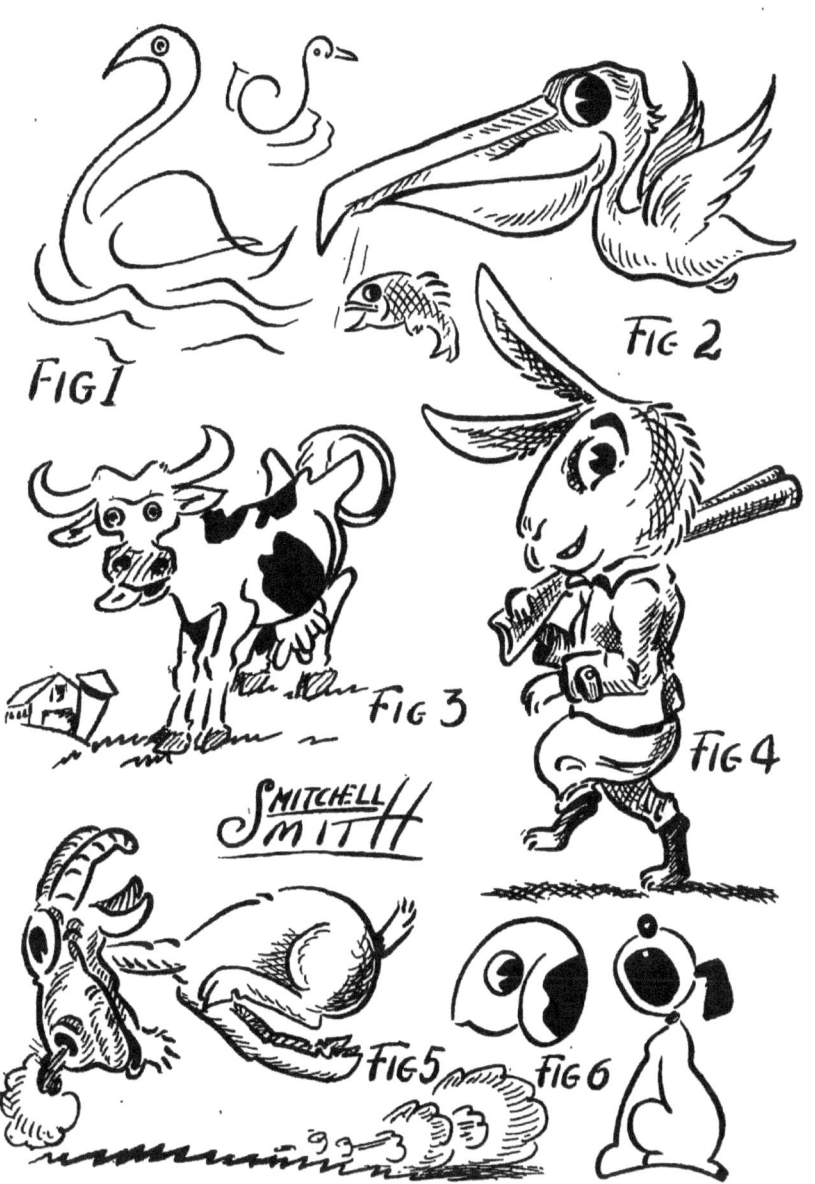

FIG 1

FIG 2

FIG 3

FIG 4

MITCHELL SMITH

FIG 5

FIG 6

PLATE 18

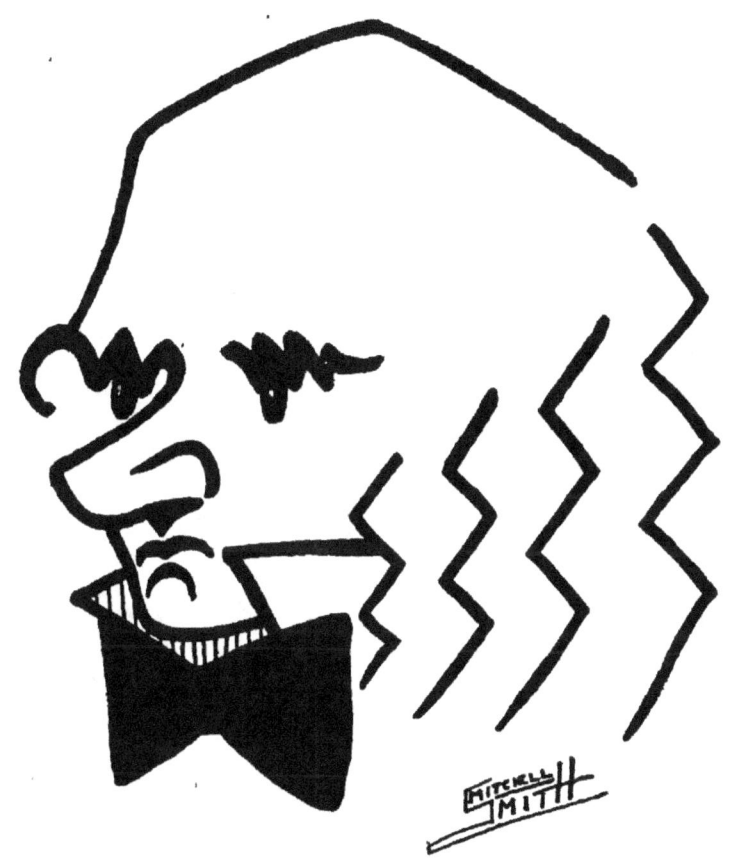

DARWIN

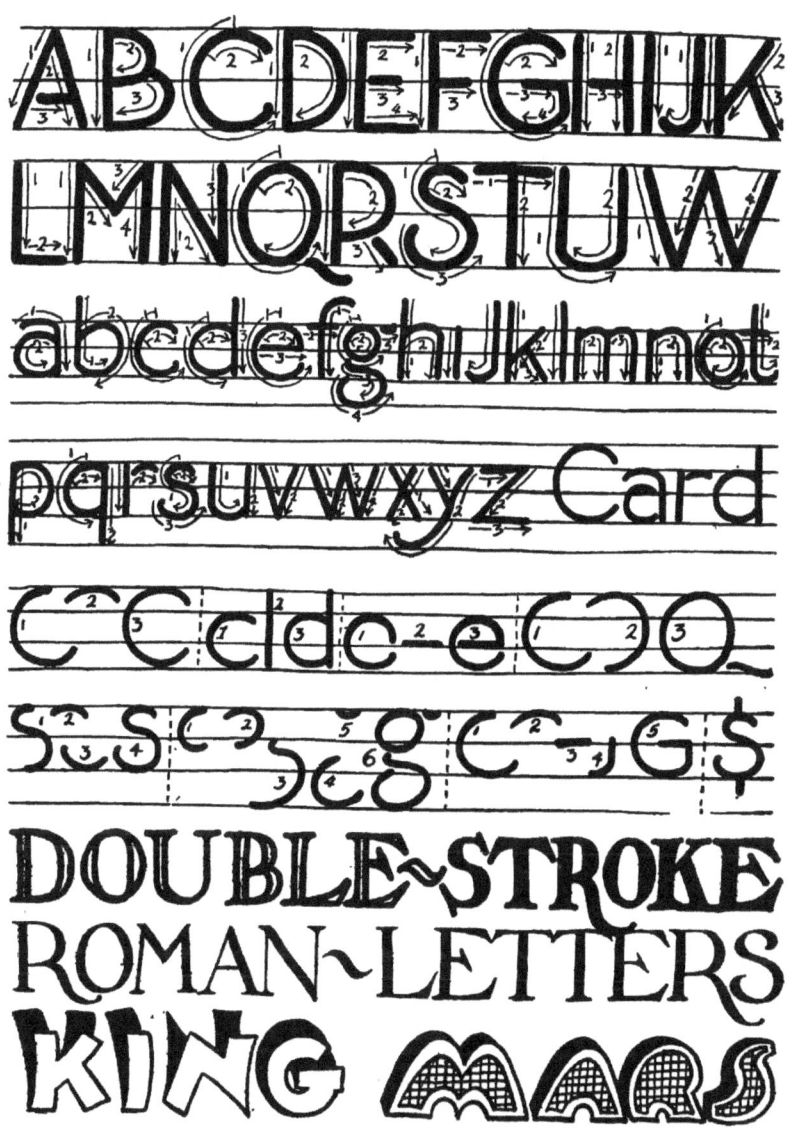

PLATE 19

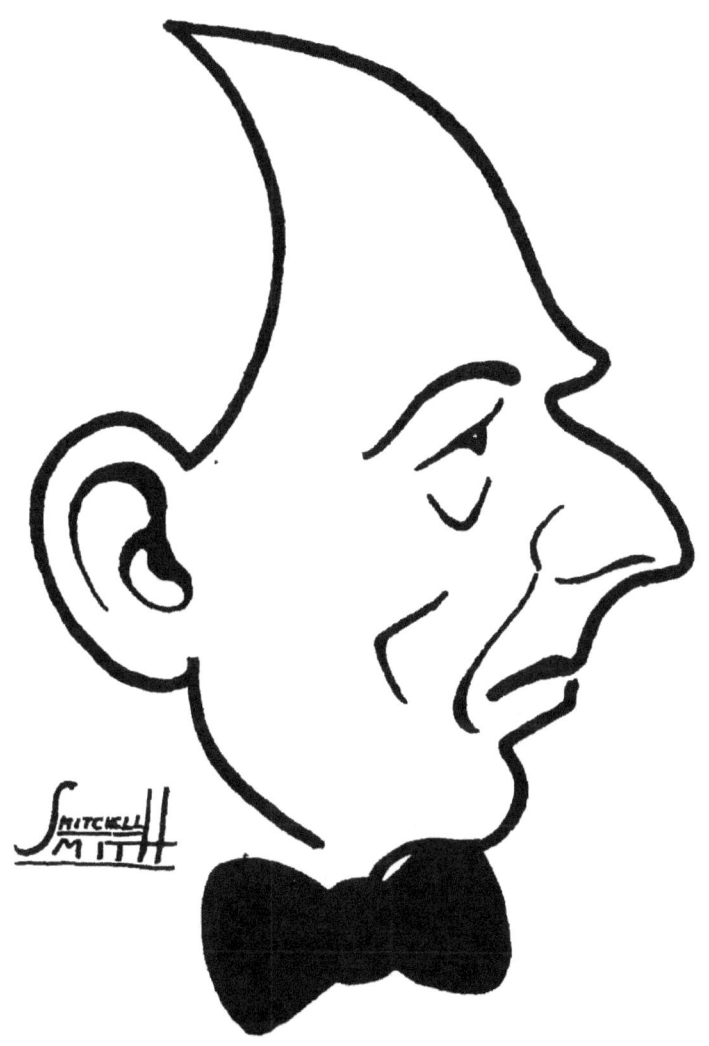

GARRETT

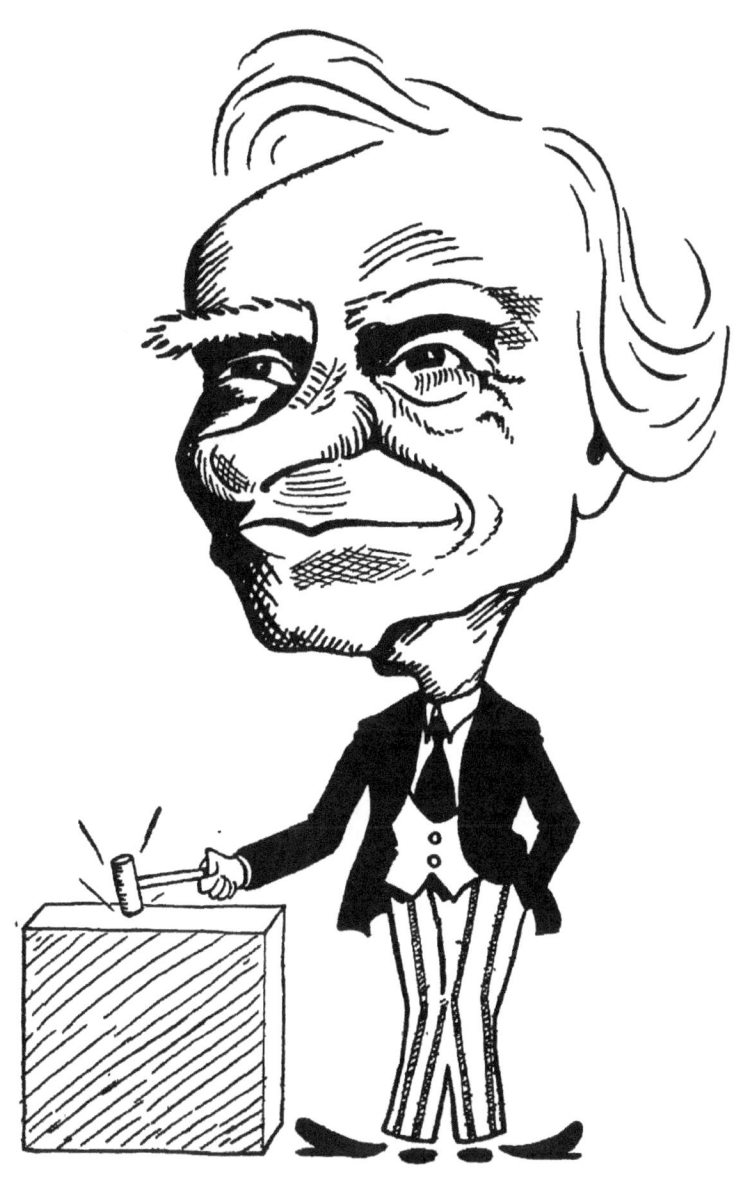

BYRNS

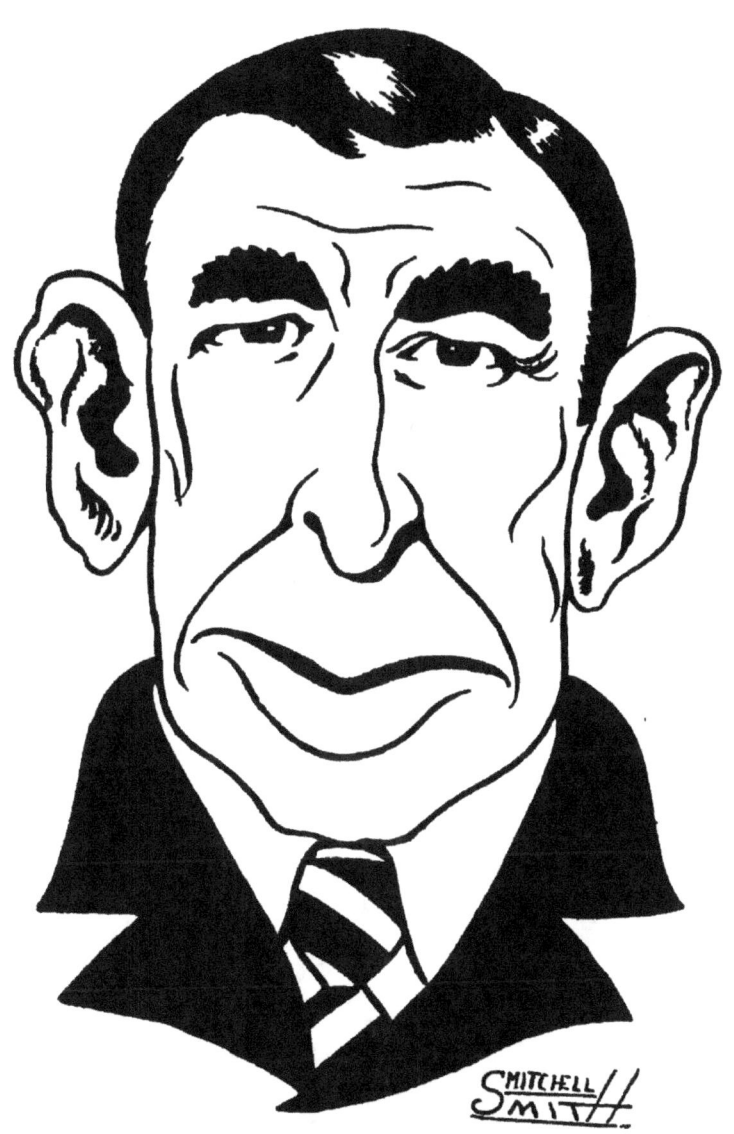

TARKINGTON

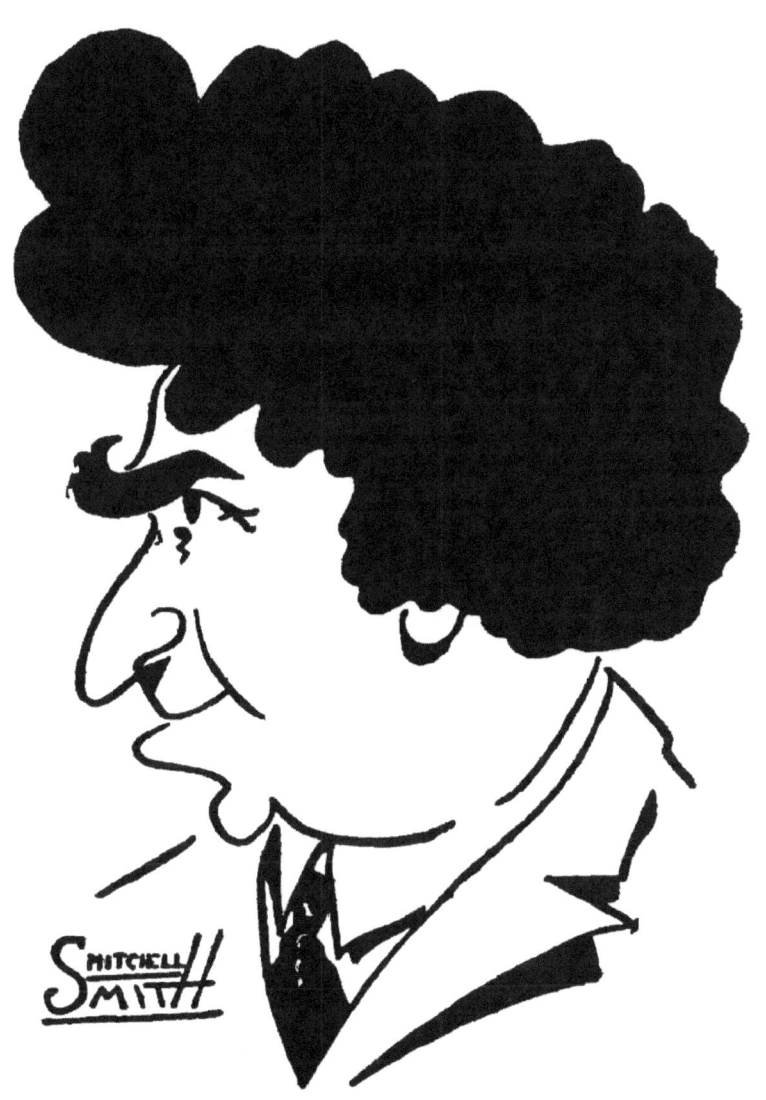

MARTINELLI

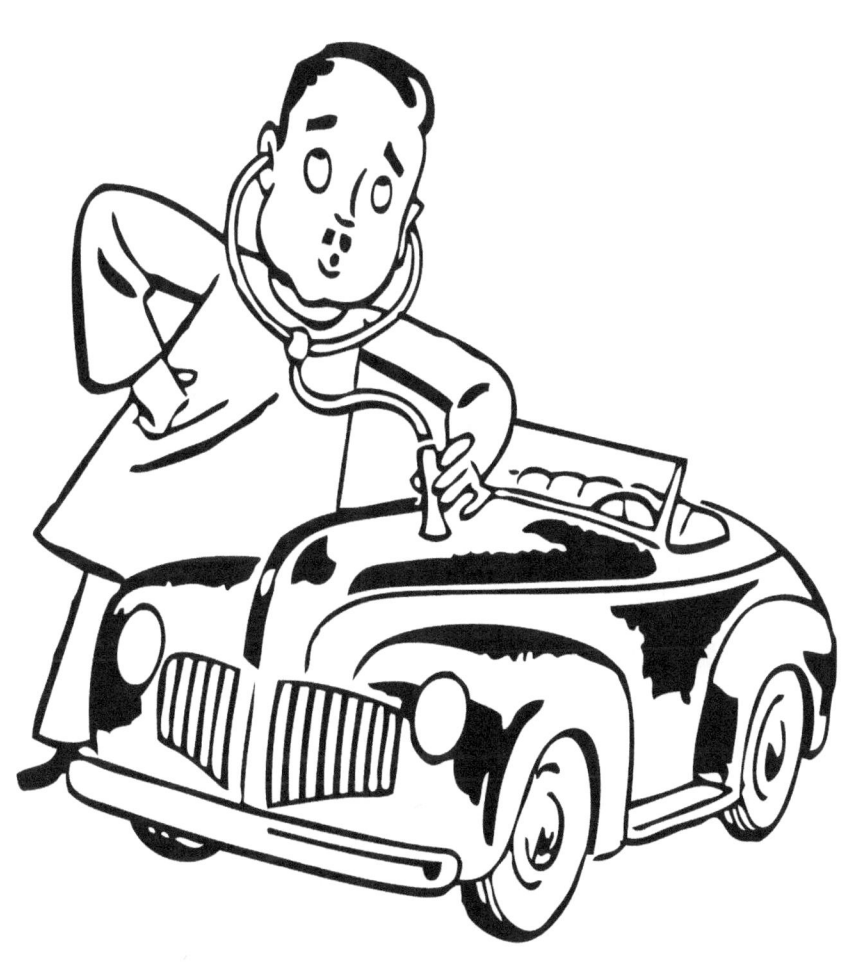

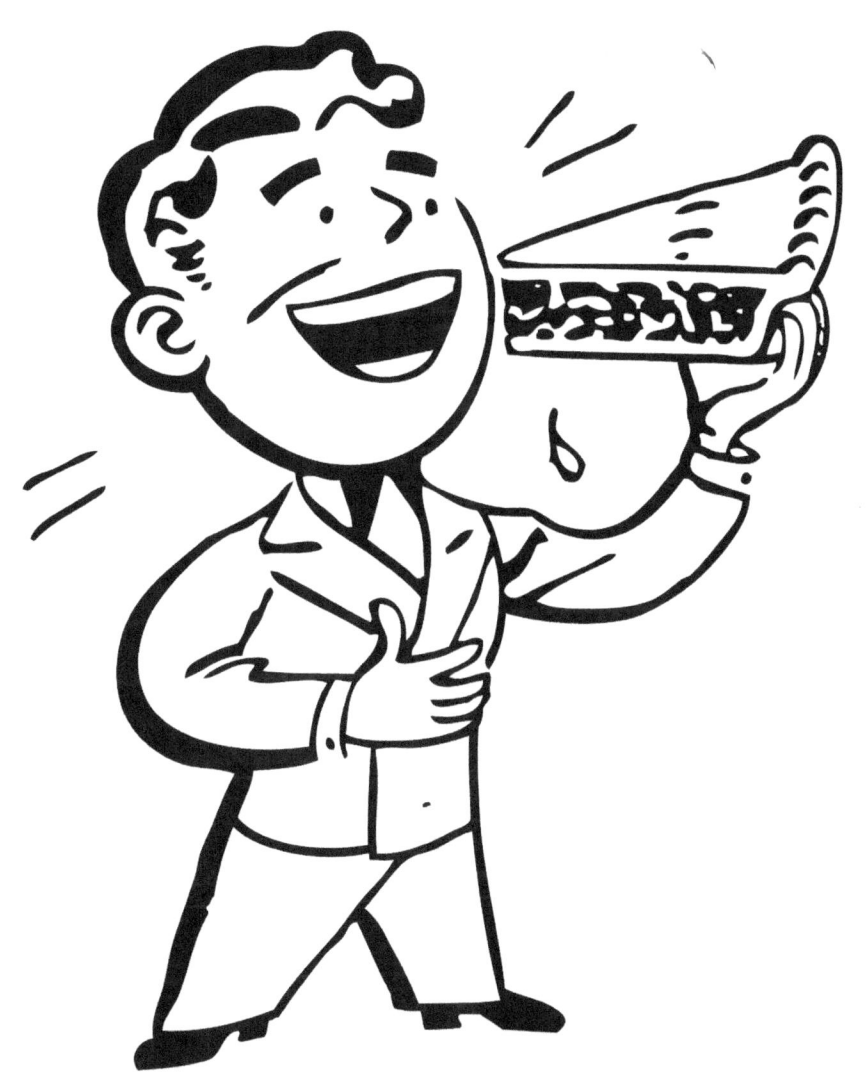

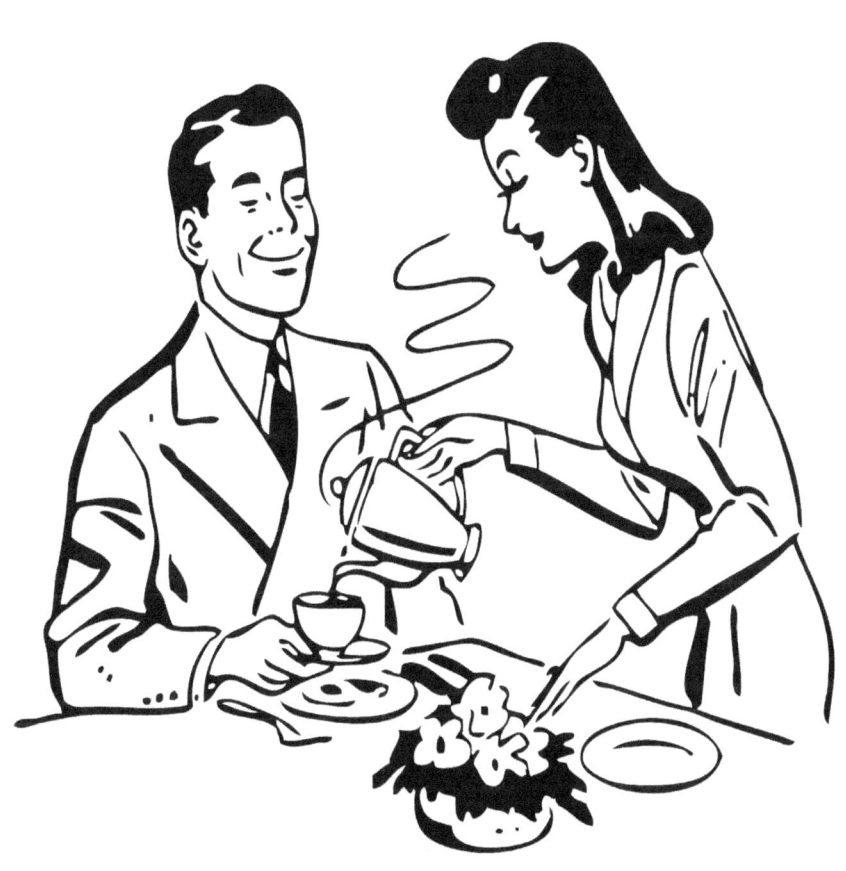

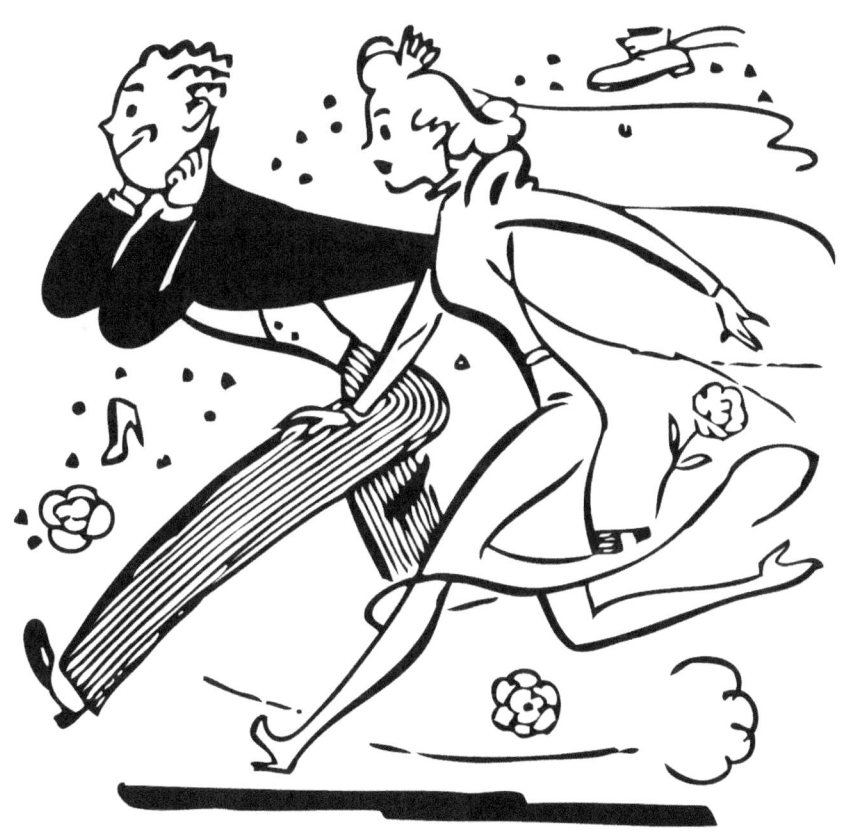

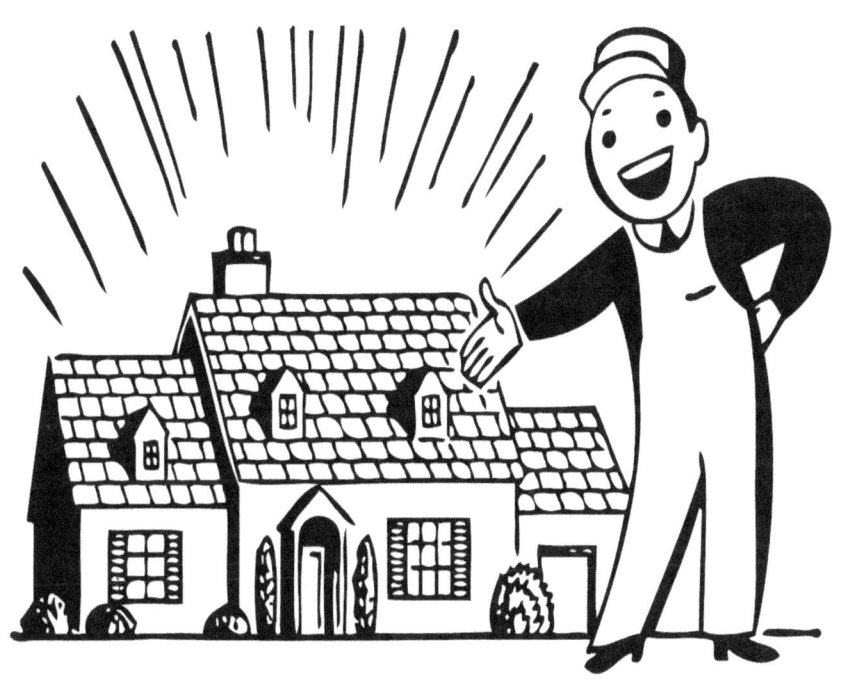

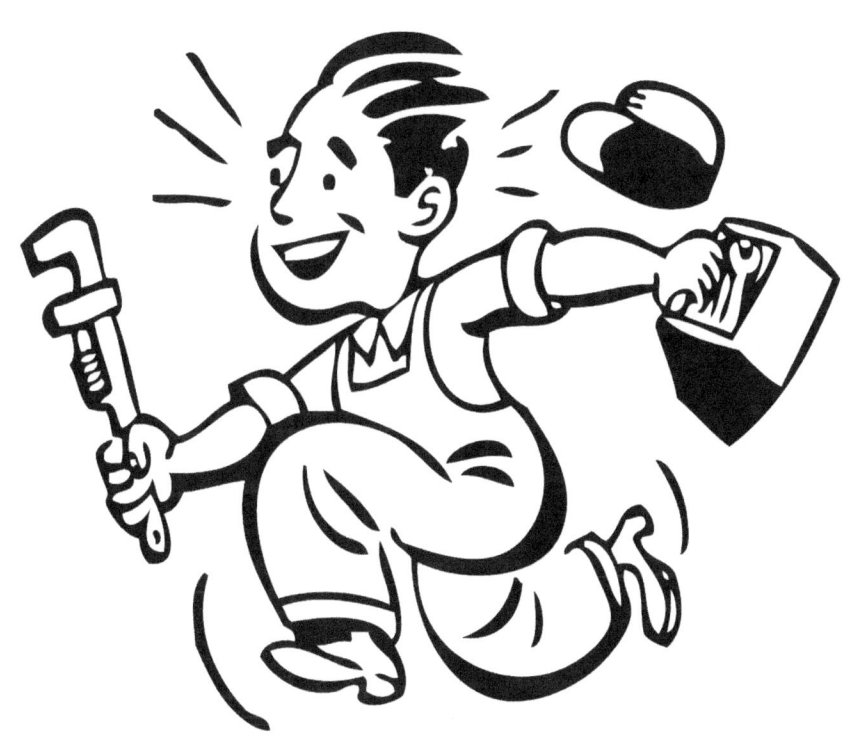

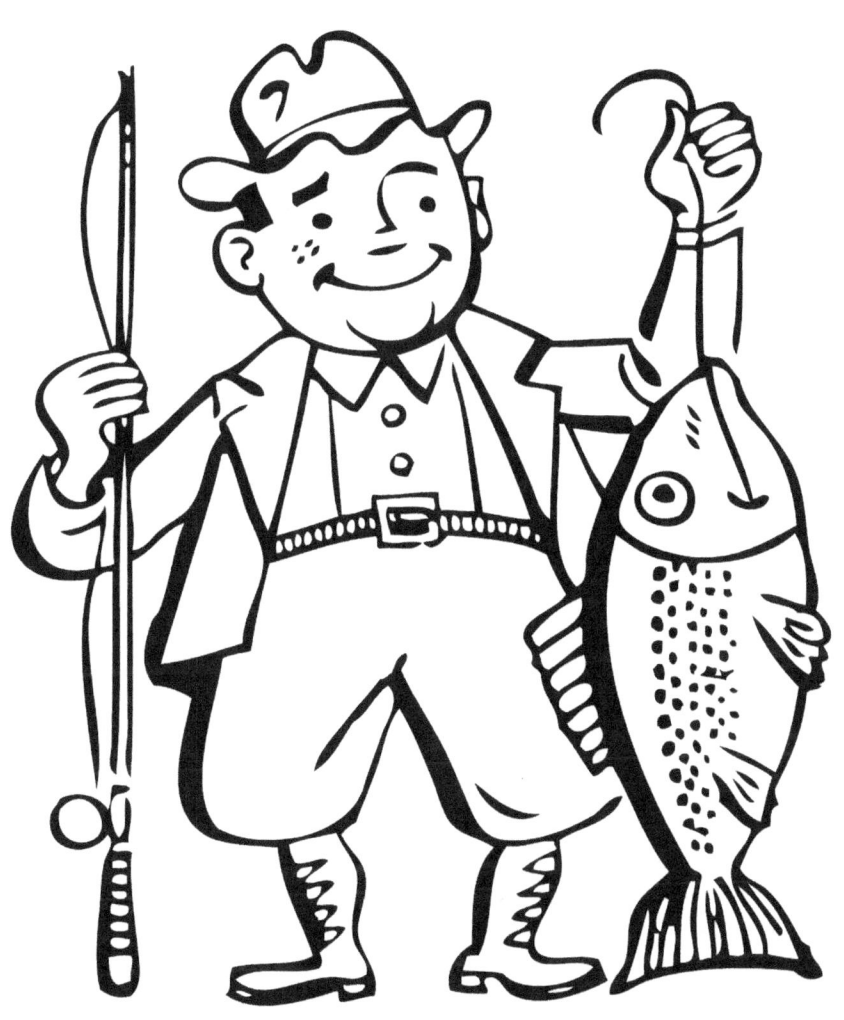

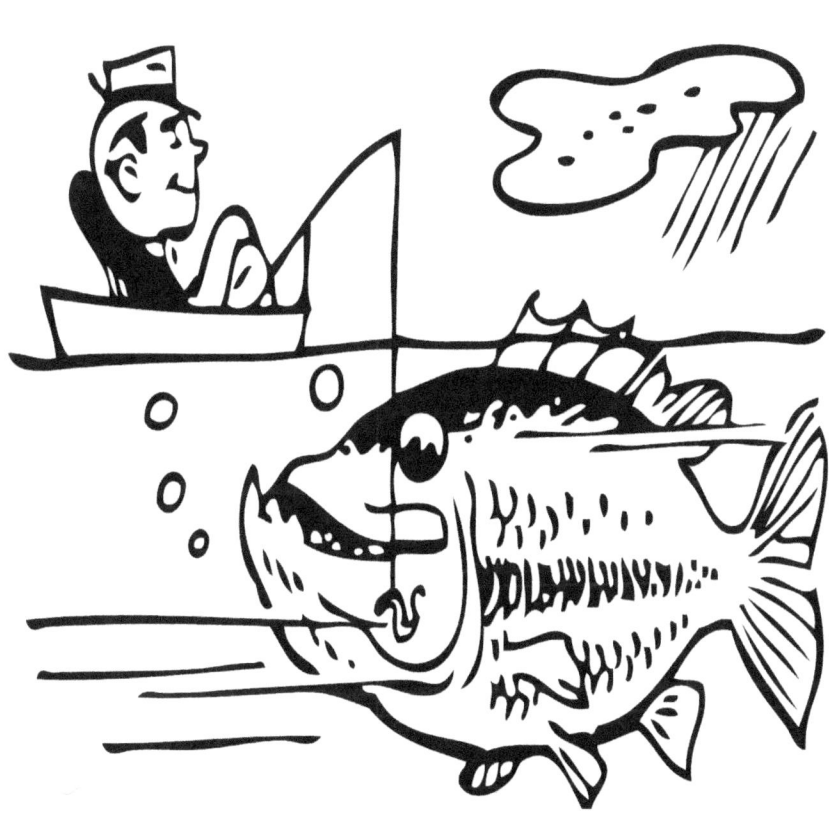

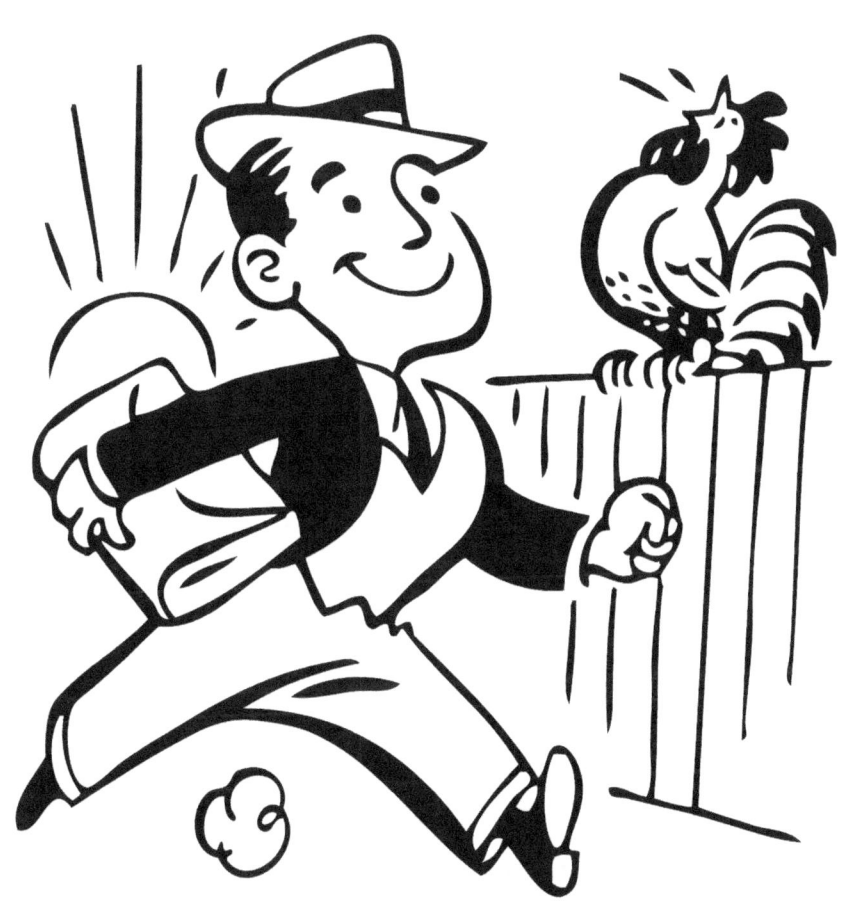

Other Coloring Books

BadASS Buttocks: Coloring Book for Adults
Silesian Folk Tales Coloring Book: Intricate Vintage Illustrations
Paisley and Patterns: Intricate Designs Coloring Book

www.ingramcontent.com/pod-product-compliance
Lightning Source LLC
Chambersburg PA
CBHW071801200526
45167CB00017B/914